GUITAR TAB

weezer

Music transcriptions by Pete Billmann and Jeff Jacobson

Editorial Assistance for Weezer by Brian Bell

ISBN 978-1-4950-6905-5

7777 W. Bluemound Rd. P.O. Box 13819 Milwaukee, WI 53213

In Australia Contact:
Hal Leonard Australia Pty. Ltd.
4 Lentara Court
Cheltenham, Victoria, 3192 Australia
Email: ausadmin@halleonard.com.au

Visit Hal Leonard Online at
www.halleonard.com

California Kids

Words and Music by Rivers Cuomo and Daniel Wilson

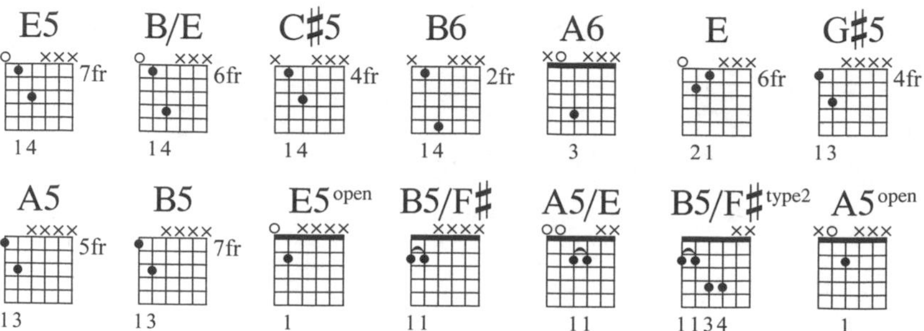

Tune down 1/2 step:
(low to high) E♭-A♭-D♭-G♭-B♭-E♭

Key of E

Intro

Slow ♩. = 75

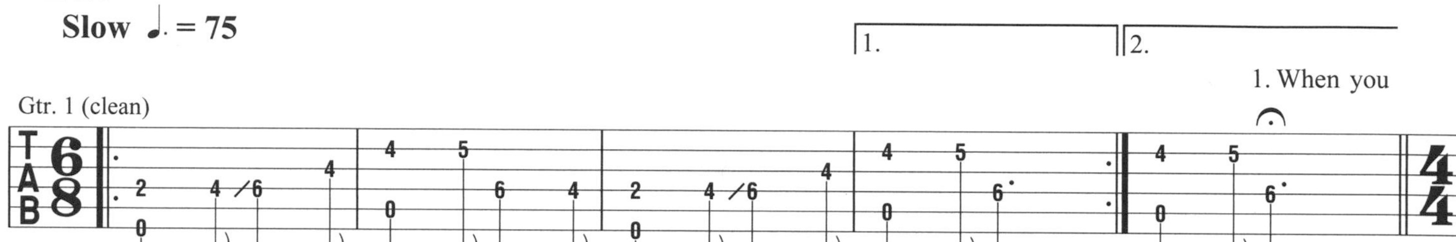

Verse

Fast ♩ = 150

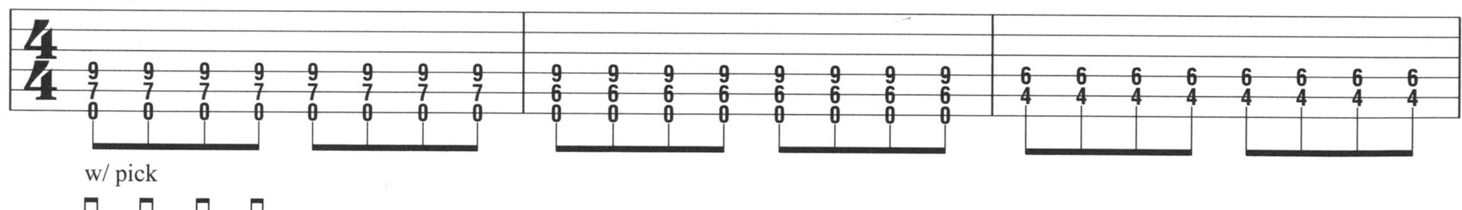

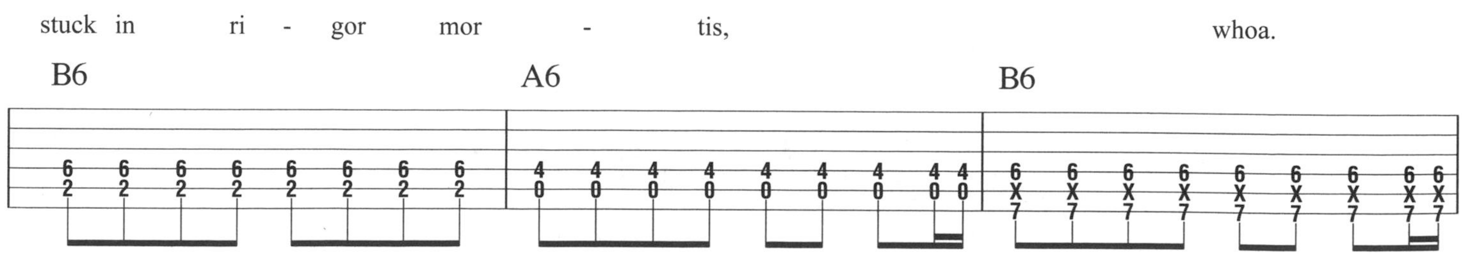

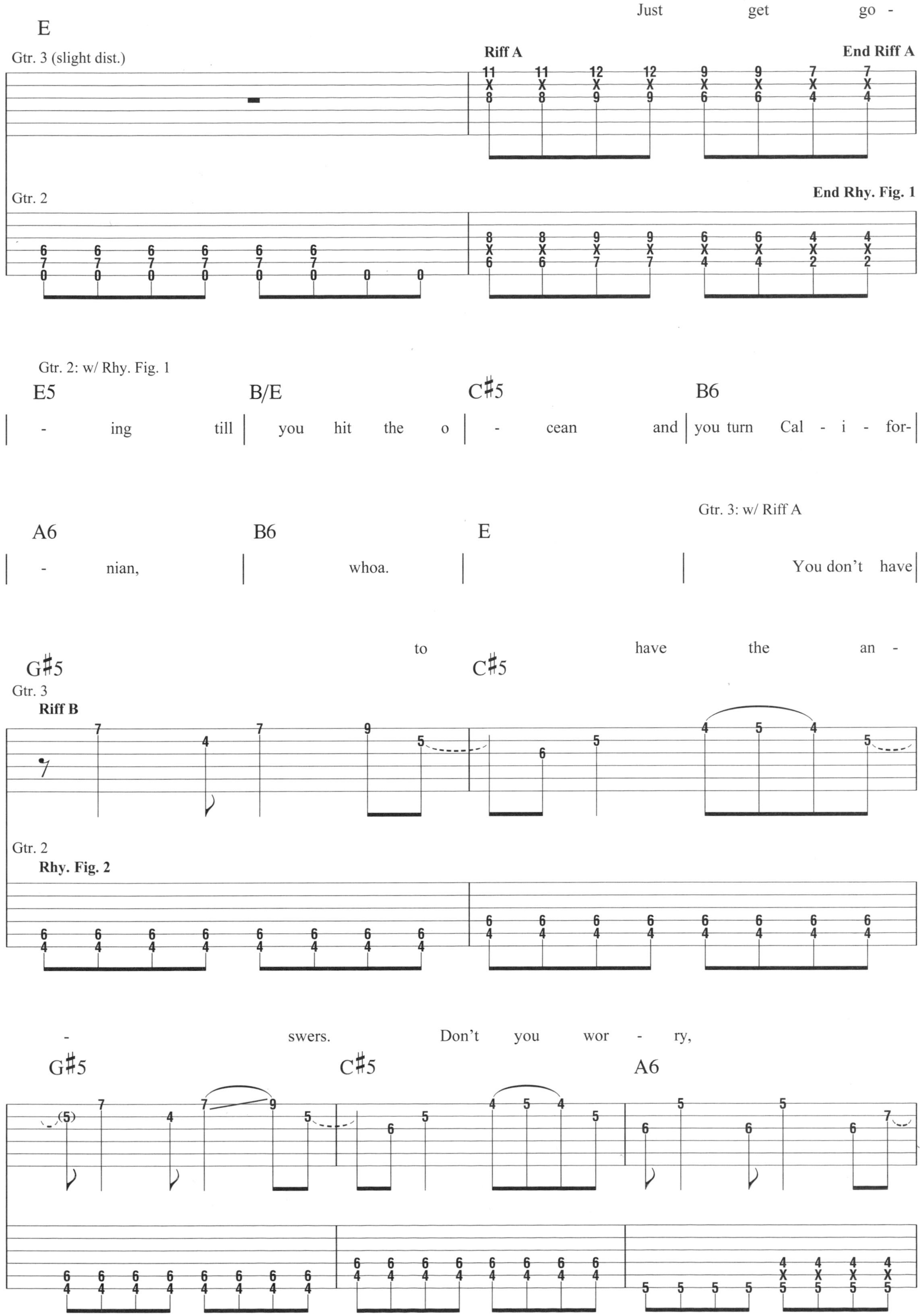
Just get go -
E
Gtr. 3 (slight dist.)
Riff A
End Riff A
Gtr. 2
End Rhy. Fig. 1
Gtr. 2: w/ Rhy. Fig. 1
E5
B/E
C♯5
B6
- ing till you hit the o - cean and you turn Cal - i - for-
A6
B6
E
Gtr. 3: w/ Riff A
- nian, whoa. You don't have
to have the an -
G♯5
C♯5
Gtr. 3
Riff B
Gtr. 2
Rhy. Fig. 2
- swers. Don't you wor - ry,
G♯5
C♯5
A6

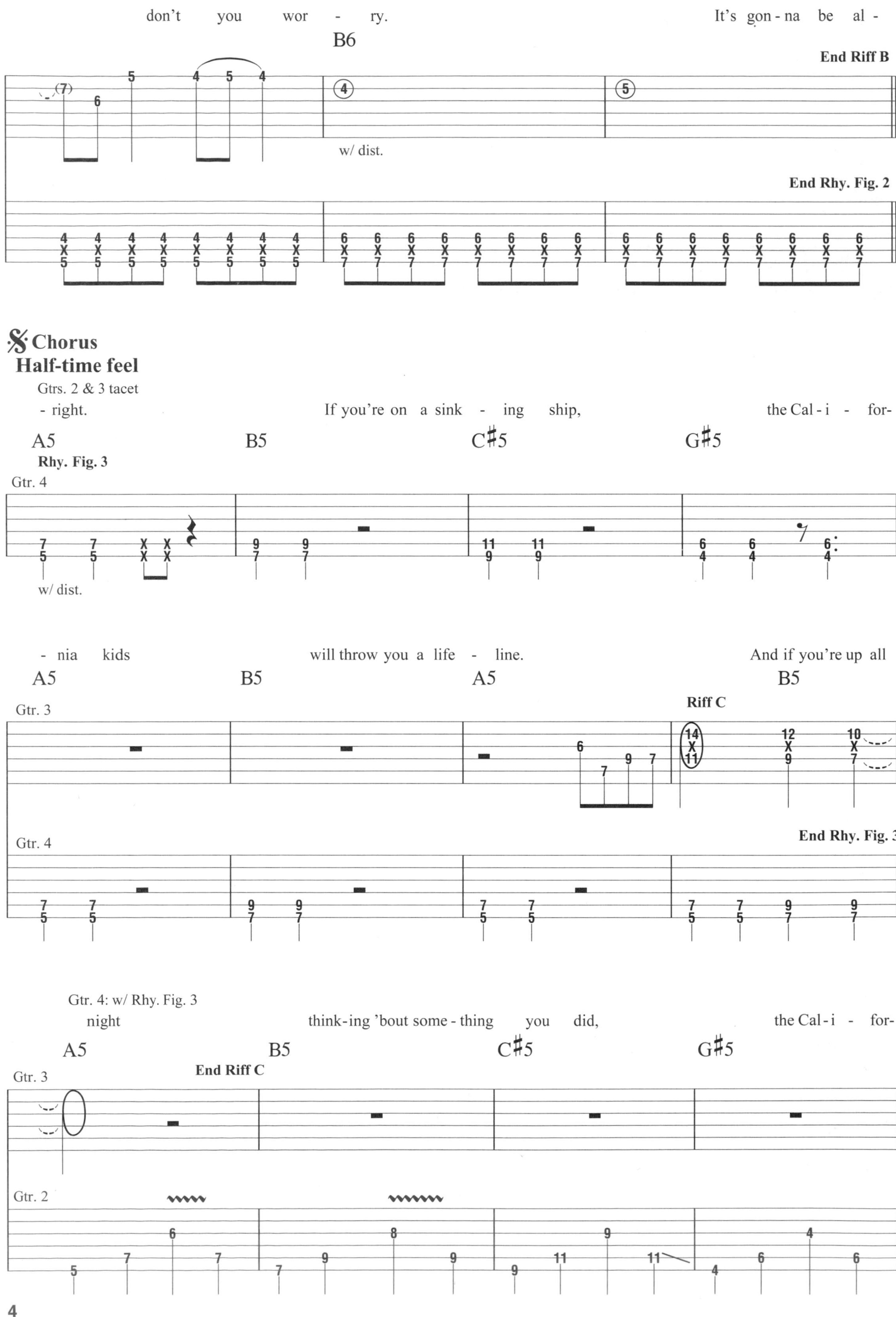

don't you wor - ry.
It's gon - na be al -
B6
End Riff B
w/ dist.
End Rhy. Fig. 2
Chorus
Half-time feel
Gtrs. 2 & 3 tacet
- right.
If you're on a sink - ing ship,
the Cal - i - for-
A5
B5
C♯5
G♯5
Rhy. Fig. 3
Gtr. 4
w/ dist.
- nia kids
will throw you a life - line.
And if you're up all
A5
B5
A5
B5
Riff C
Gtr. 3
Gtr. 4
End Rhy. Fig. 3
Gtr. 4: w/ Rhy. Fig. 3
night
think-ing 'bout some - thing you did,
the Cal - i - for-
A5
B5
C♯5
G♯5
End Riff C
Gtr. 3
Gtr. 2

To Coda 𝄌

End half-time feel

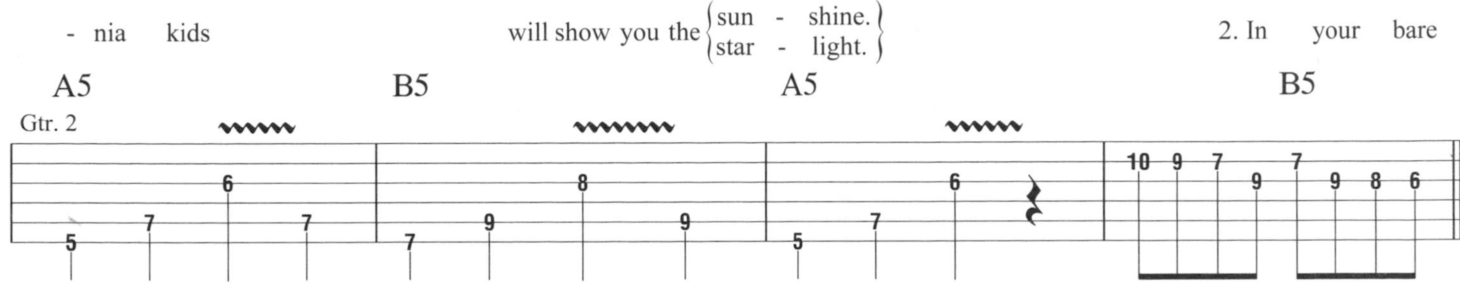

Verse

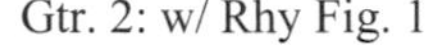

feet in mid - Jan - u - ar - y, swim-ming in the mys-

E5 B/E C♯5 B6

Gtr. 3

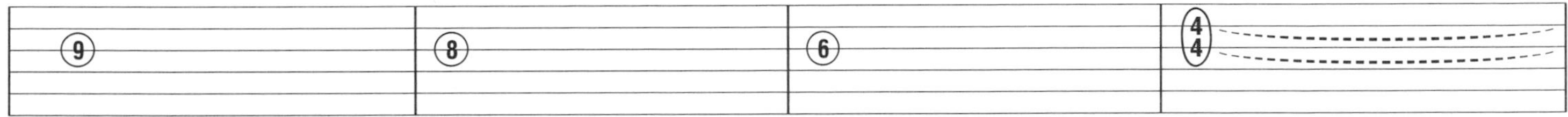

Gtr. 2: w/ Rhy. Fig. 2
Gtr. 3: w/ Riff B

G♯5 C♯5 G♯5 C♯5

| - ing | al - most ev | - 'ry - thing. | Don't you wor- |

D.S. al Coda

A6 B6

| - ry, | don't you wor | - ry. | It's gon - na be al - ||

𝄌 Coda

Guitar Solo

A5

Gtr. 5 (dist.)

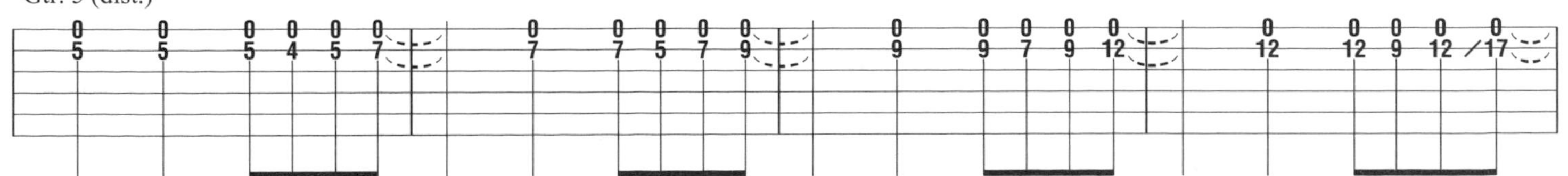

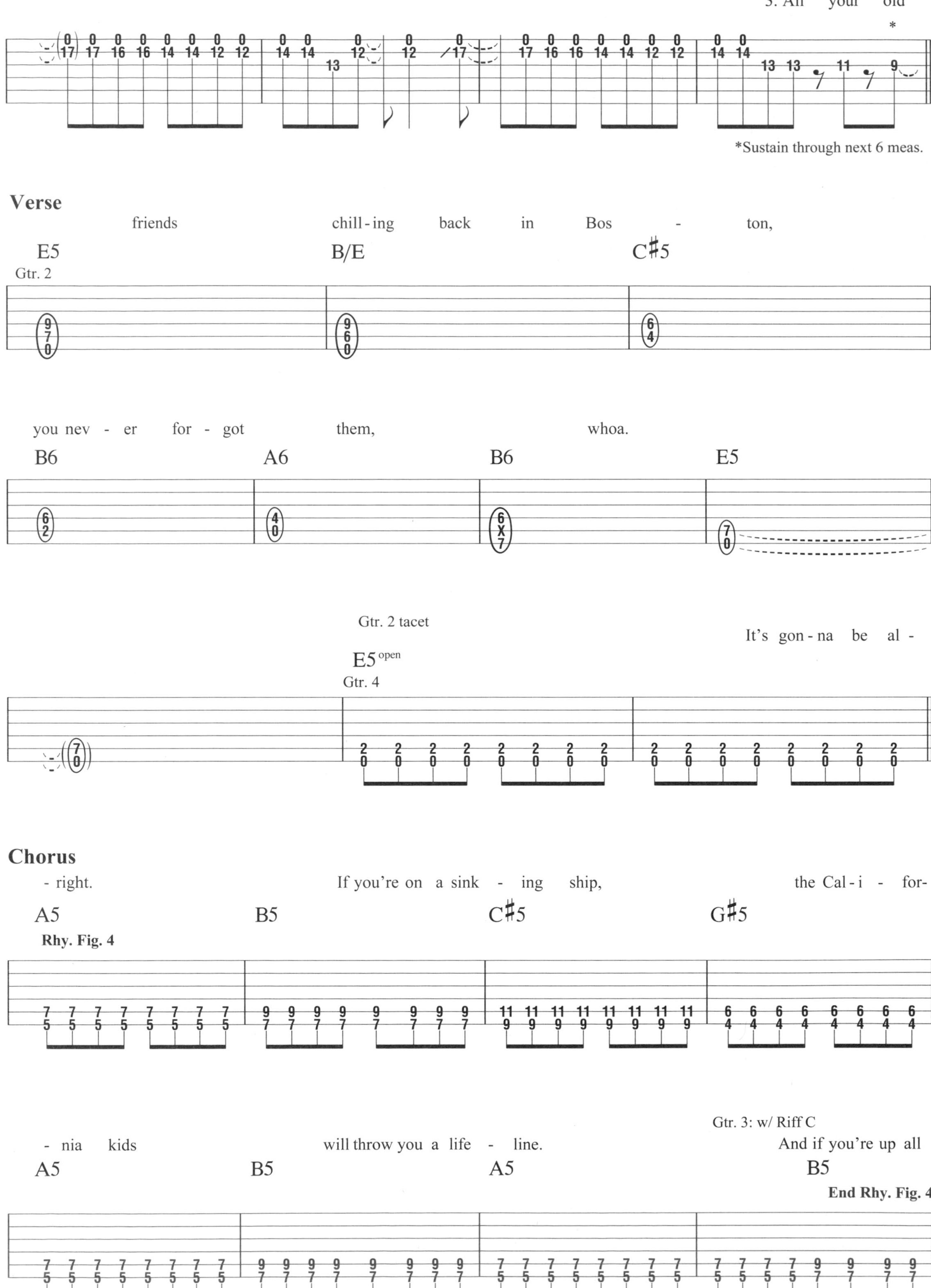

3. All your old
*Sustain through next 6 meas.
Verse
friends chill-ing back in Bos - ton,
E5 B/E C♯5
Gtr. 2
you nev - er for - got them, whoa.
B6 A6 B6 E5
Gtr. 2 tacet
It's gon-na be al -
E5 open
Gtr. 4
Chorus
- right. If you're on a sink - ing ship, the Cal-i - for-
A5 B5 C♯5 G♯5
Rhy. Fig. 4
- nia kids will throw you a life - line.
Gtr. 3: w/ Riff C
And if you're up all
A5 B5 A5 B5
End Rhy. Fig. 4

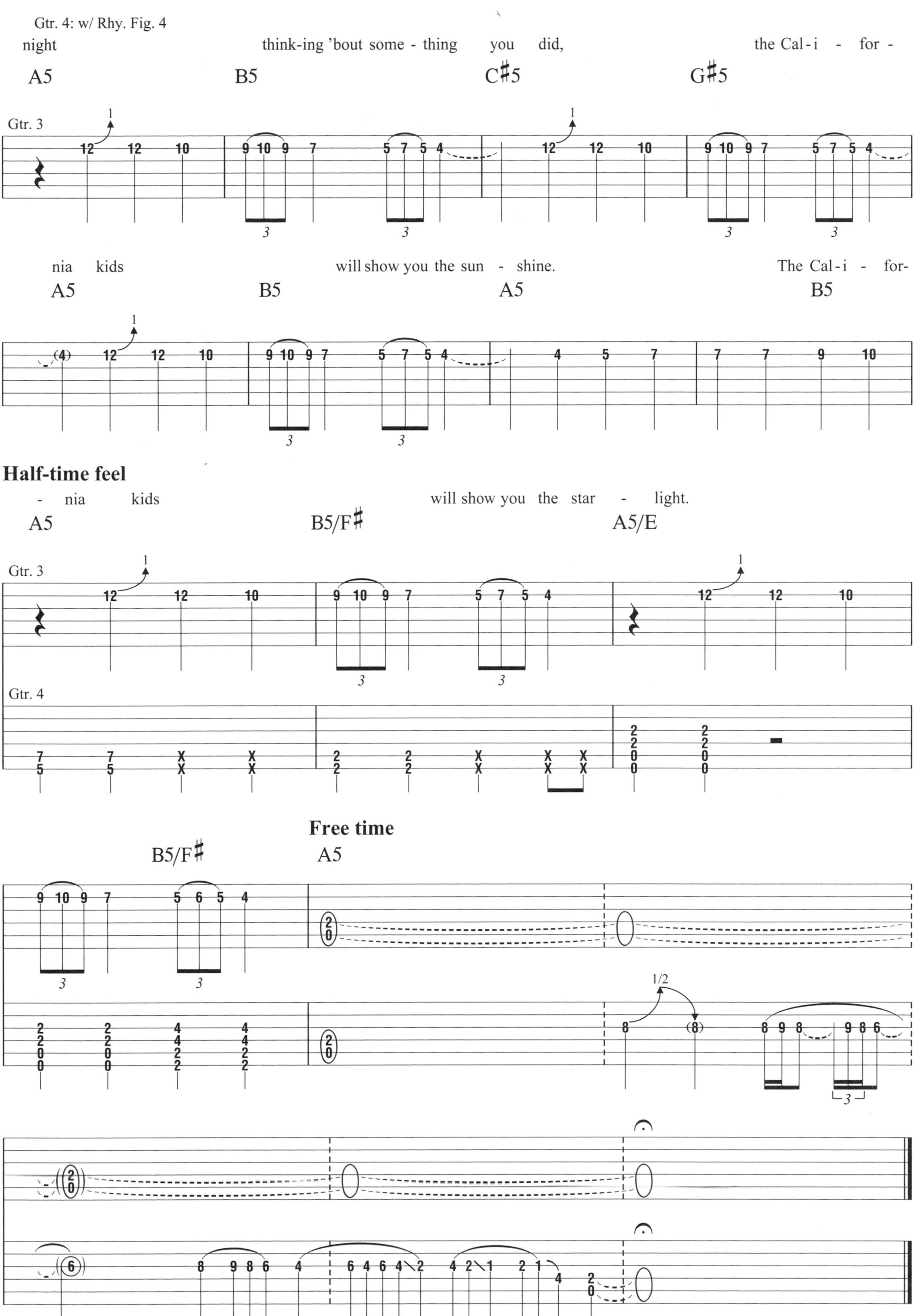
Gtr. 4: w/ Rhy. Fig. 4
night thinking 'bout something you did, the Cali - for -
A5 B5 C♯5 G♯5
Gtr. 3
nia kids will show you the sun - shine. The Cal-i - for-
A5 B5 A5 B5
Half-time feel
- nia kids will show you the star - light.
A5 B5/F♯ A5/E
Gtr. 3
Gtr. 4
B5/F♯
Free time
A5

Wind in Our Sail

Words and Music by Rivers Cuomo, Kenneth Scott Chesak and Ryan Spraker

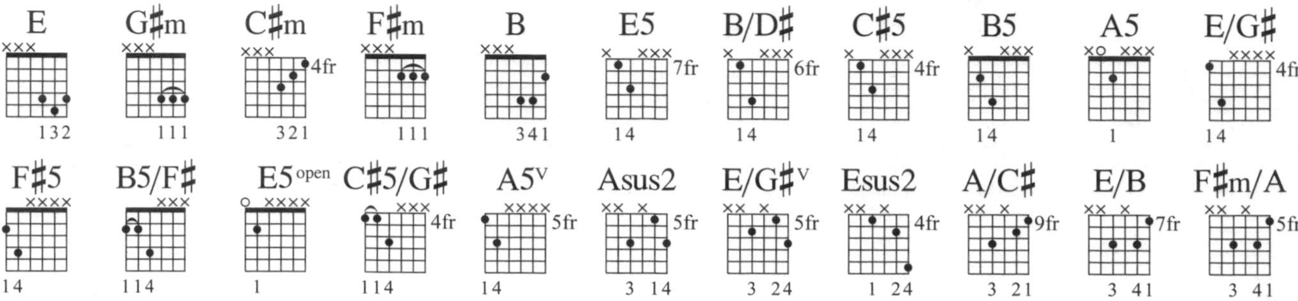

Tune down 1/2 step:
(low to high) E♭-A♭-D♭-G♭-B♭-E♭

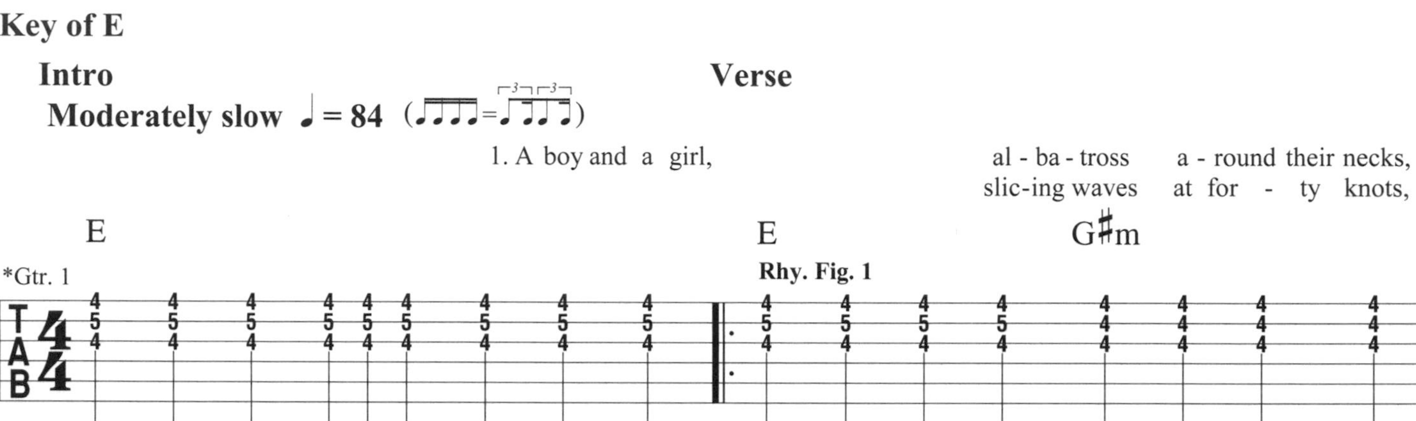

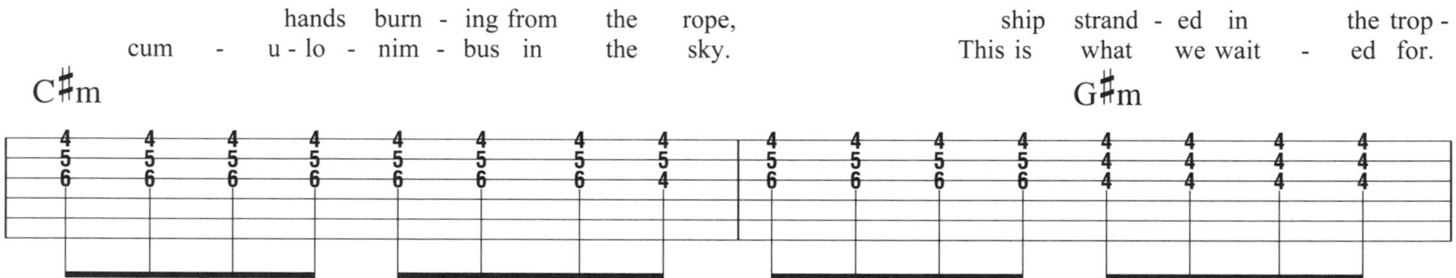

Gtr. 1: w/ Rhy. Fig. 1

- ics. A-cid - i - fi - ca - tion wiped out the ti - ger shark.

And now there's no more hy-per-ven-tal-at-ing in wheel-chairs, we're gon-na

F♯m B E G♯m

End Rhy. Fig. 1

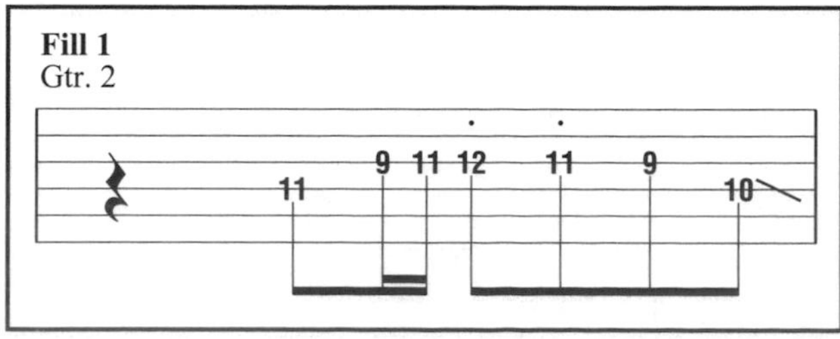

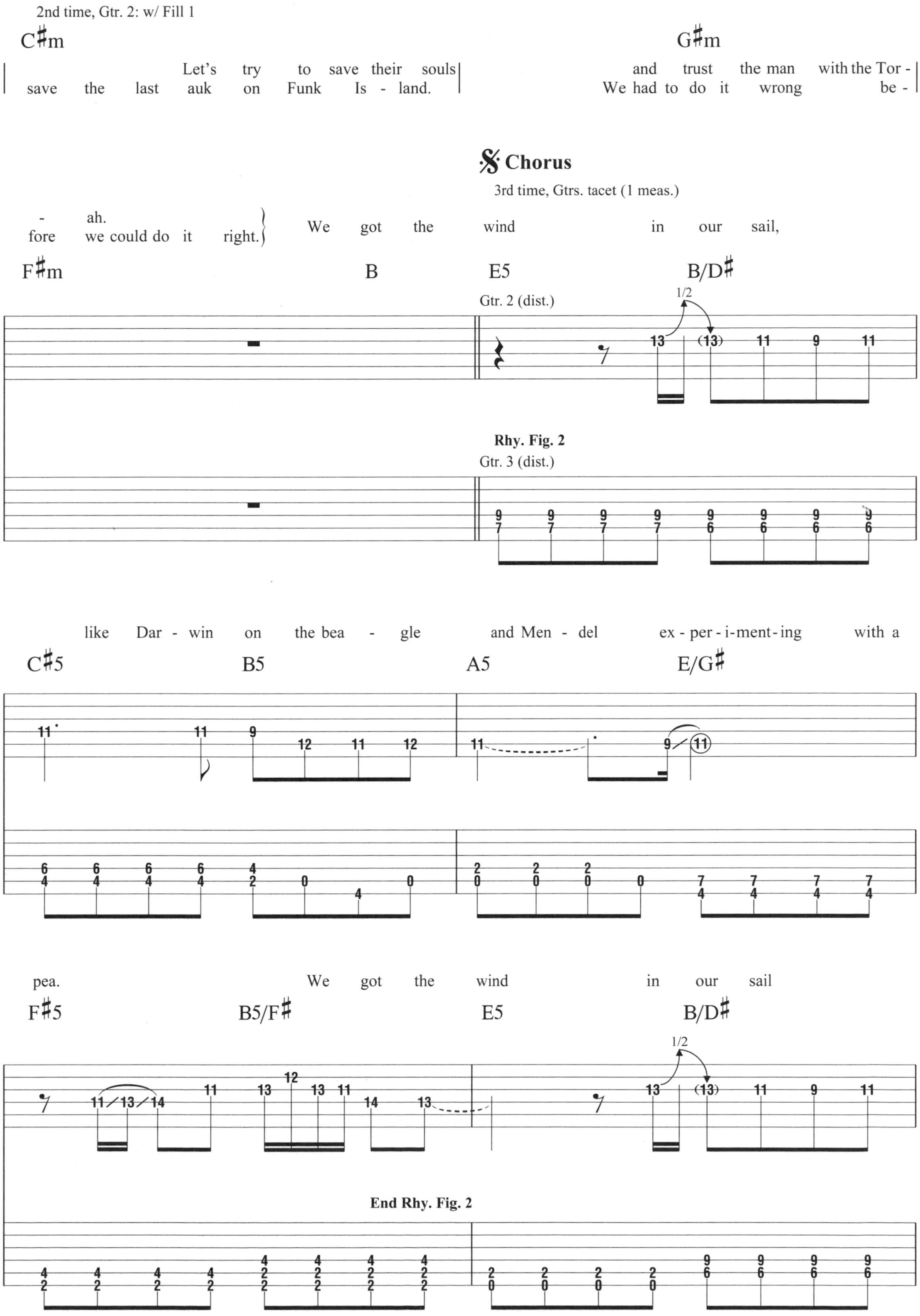

2nd time, Gtr. 2: w/ Fill 1

Let's try to save their souls
save the last auk on Funk Is - land.

G#m

and trust the man with the Tor -
We had to do it wrong be -

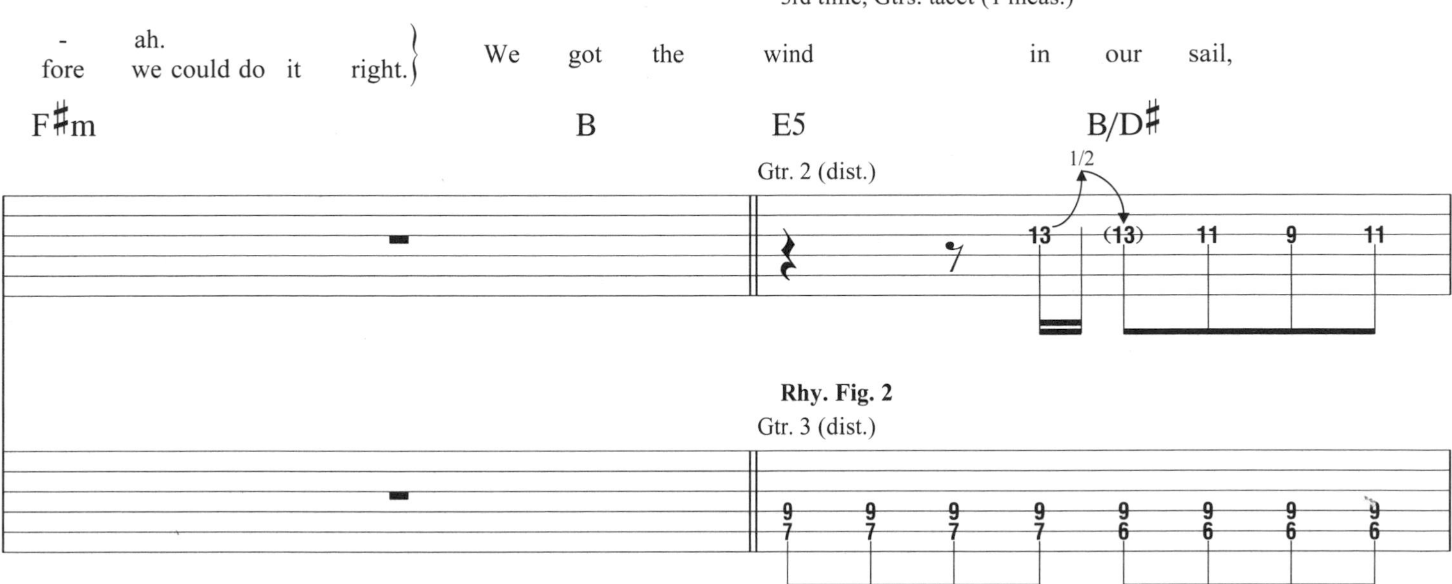

like Dar - win on the bea - gle and Men - del ex - per - i - ment - ing with a

C#5 B5 A5 E/G#

pea. We got the wind in our sail

F#5 B5/F# E5 B/D#

1/2

End Rhy. Fig. 2

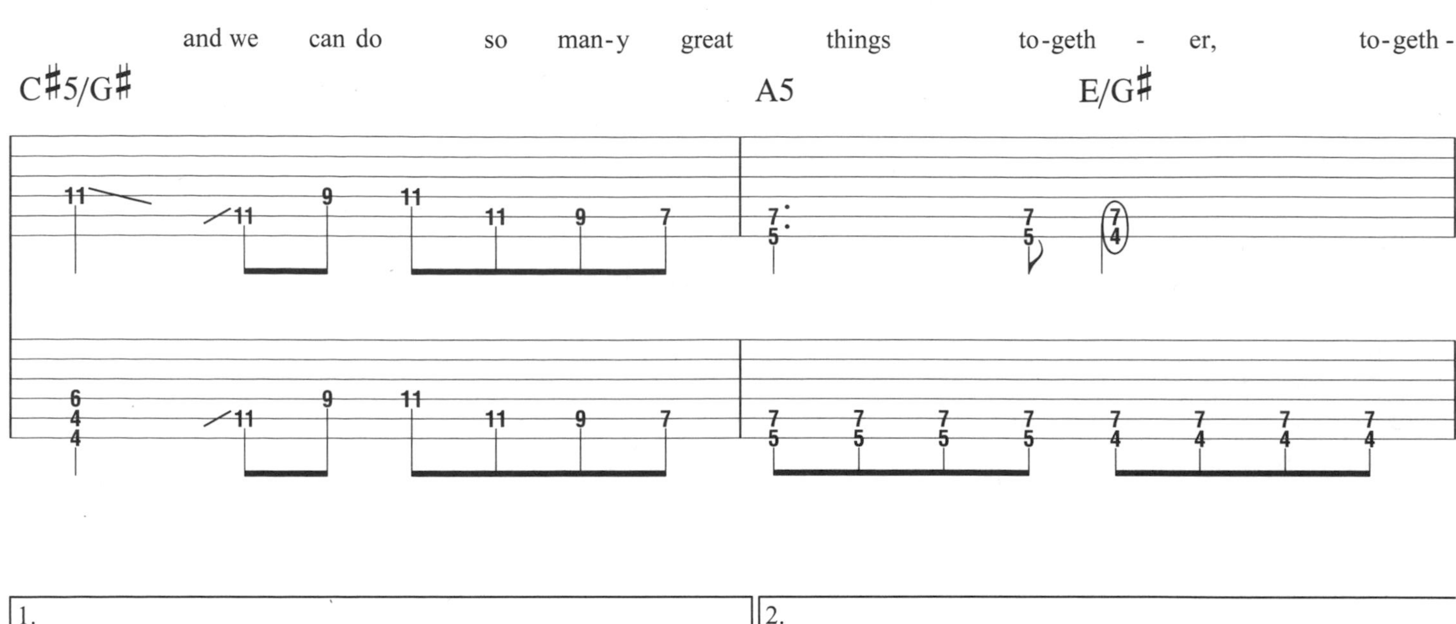

and we can do so man-y great things to-geth - er, to-geth -
C♯5/G♯
A5
E/G♯

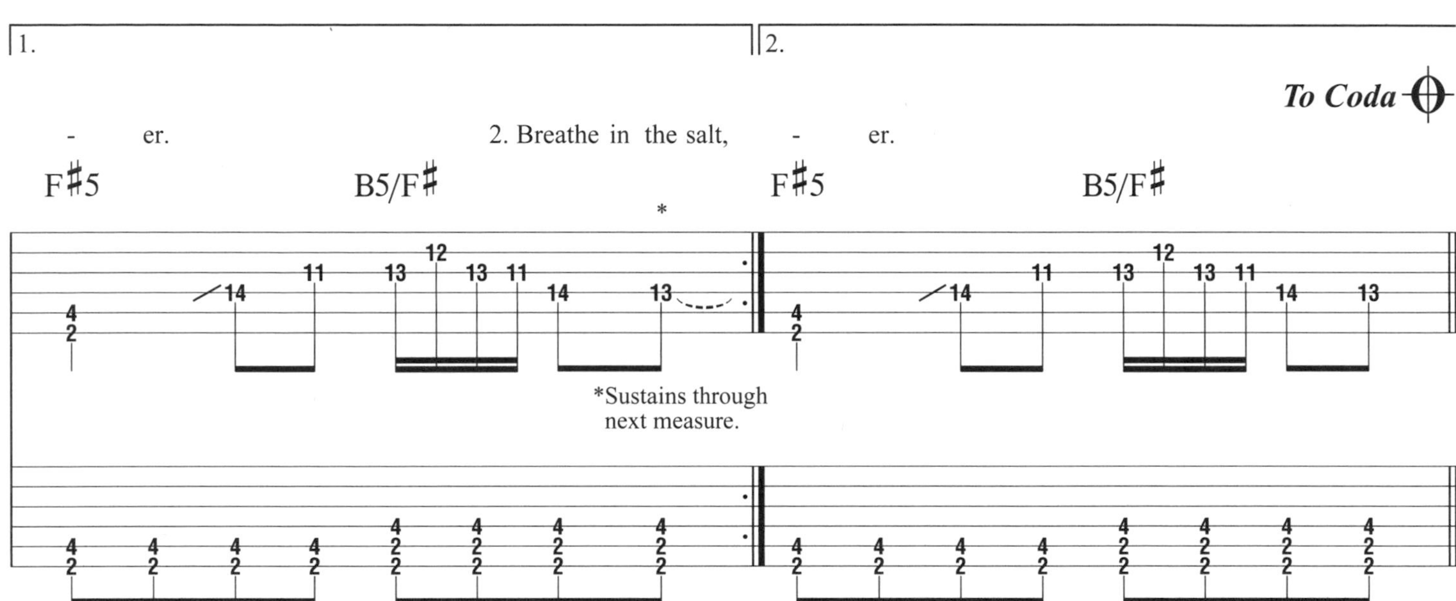

1.
2.
To Coda
- er. 2. Breathe in the salt, - er.
F♯5
B5/F♯
F♯5
B5/F♯
*Sustains through next measure.

Bridge

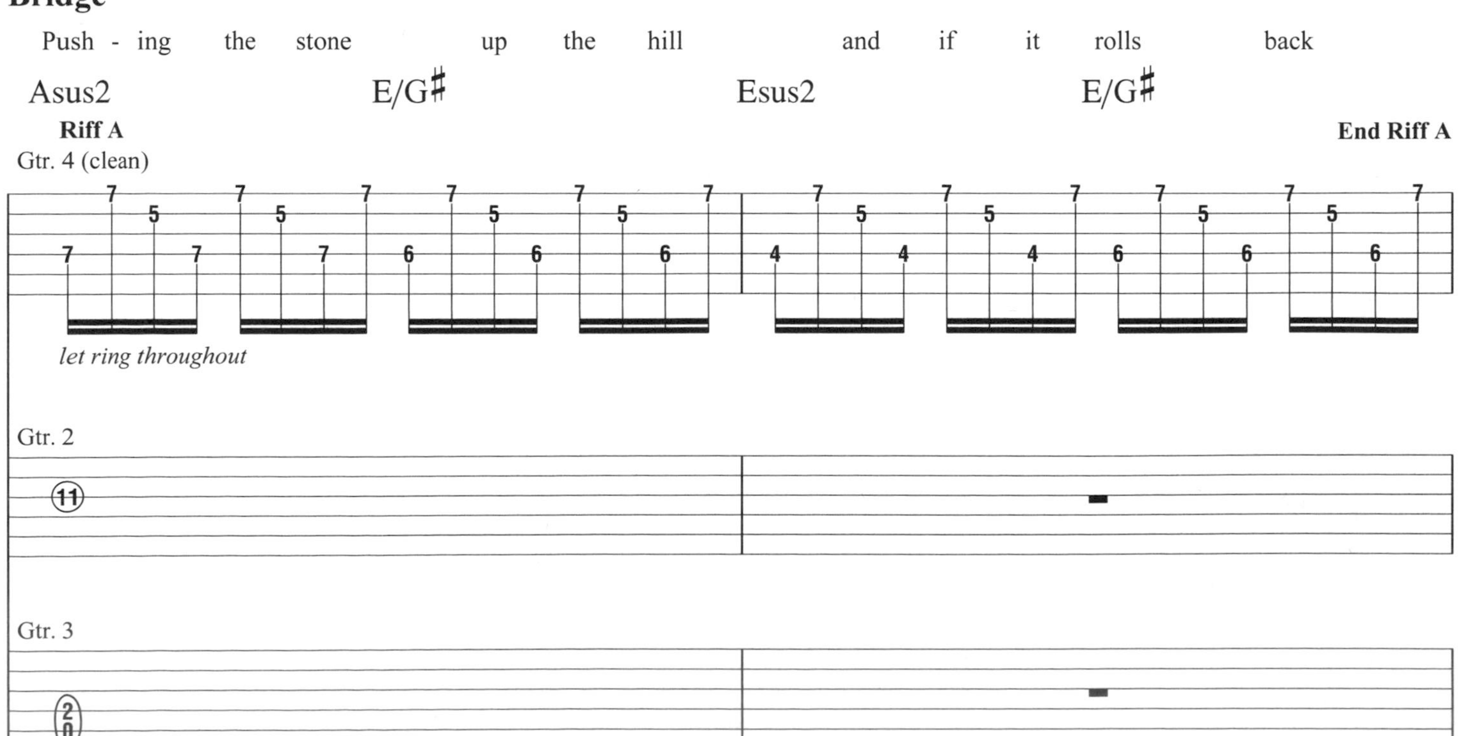

Push - ing the stone up the hill and if it rolls back
Asus2
E/G♯
Esus2
E/G♯
Riff A
End Riff A
Gtr. 4 (clean)
let ring throughout
Gtr. 2
Gtr. 3

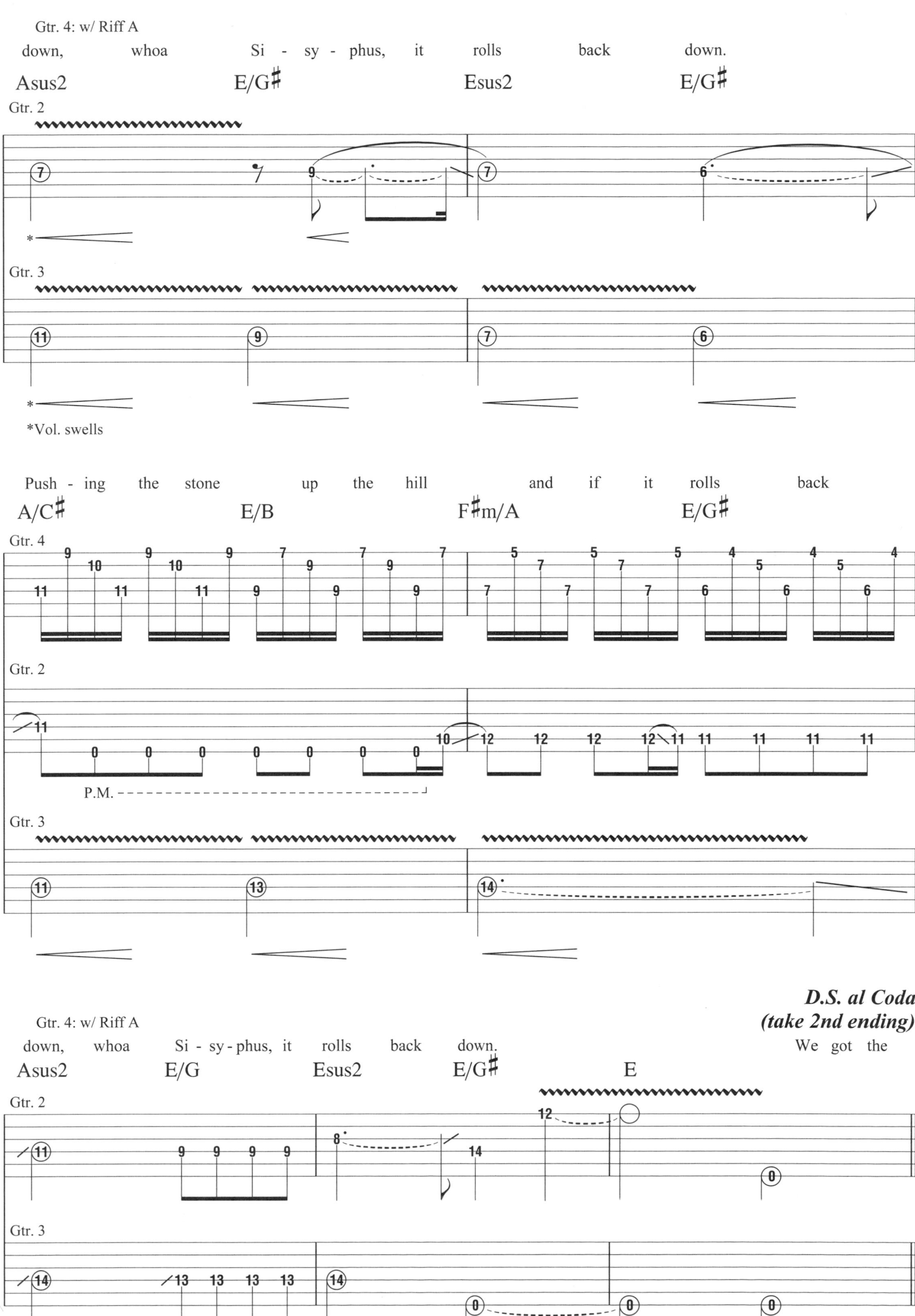
Gtr. 4: w/ Riff A
down, whoa Si - sy - phus, it rolls back down.
Asus2 E/G♯ Esus2 E/G♯
Gtr. 2
Gtr. 3
*Vol. swells
Push - ing the stone up the hill and if it rolls back
A/C♯ E/B F♯m/A E/G♯
Gtr. 4
Gtr. 2
P.M.
Gtr. 3
D.S. al Coda
(take 2nd ending)
Gtr. 4: w/ Riff A
down, whoa Si - sy - phus, it rolls back down. We got the
Asus2 E/G Esus2 E/G♯ E
Gtr. 2
Gtr. 3

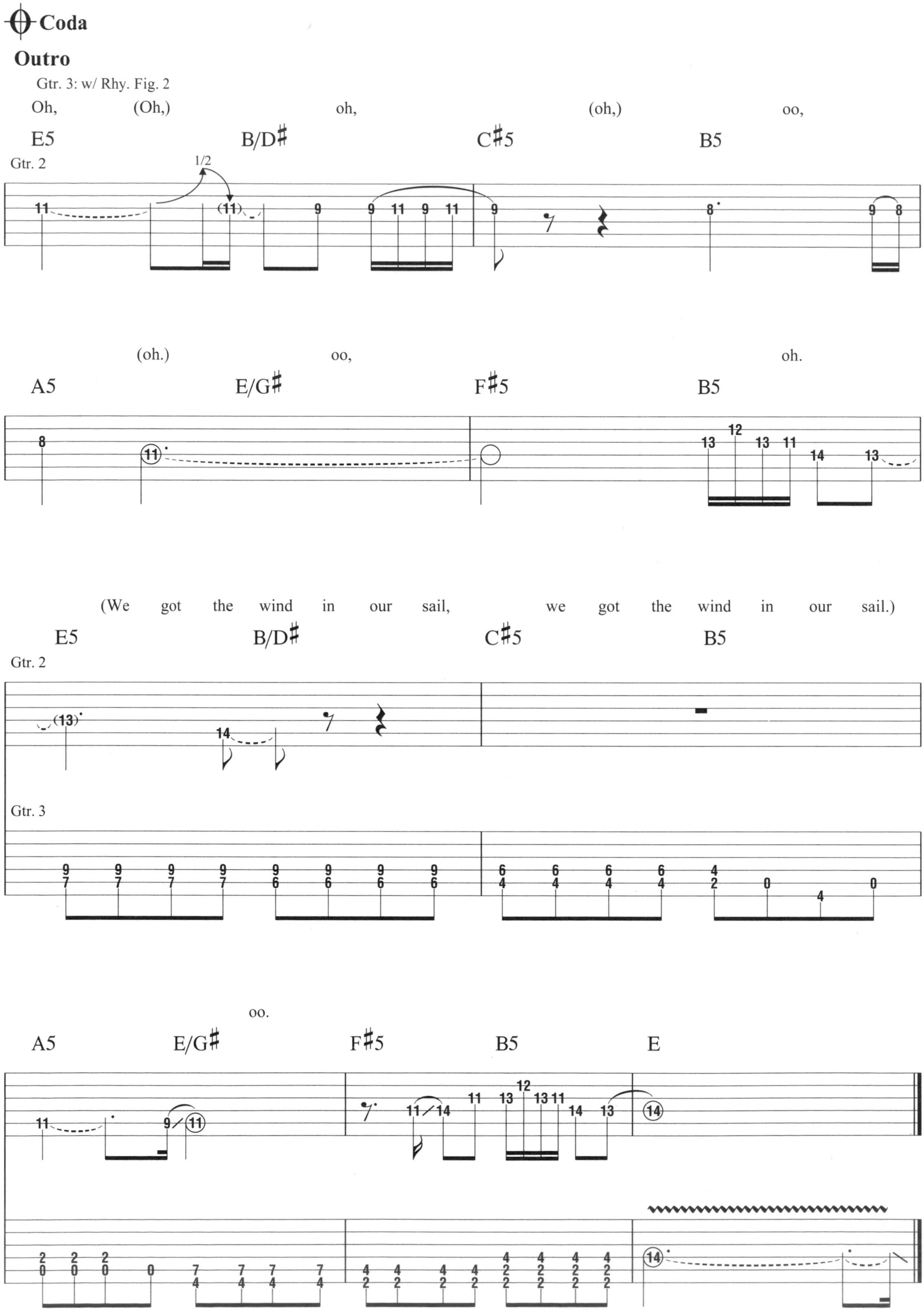

Coda

Outro

Gtr. 3: w/ Rhy. Fig. 2

Oh, (Oh,) oh, (oh,) oo,

E5 B/D# C#5 B5

Gtr. 2

(oh.) oo, oh.

A5 E/G# F#5 B5

(We got the wind in our sail, we got the wind in our sail.)

E5 B/D# C#5 B5

Gtr. 2

Gtr. 3

oo.

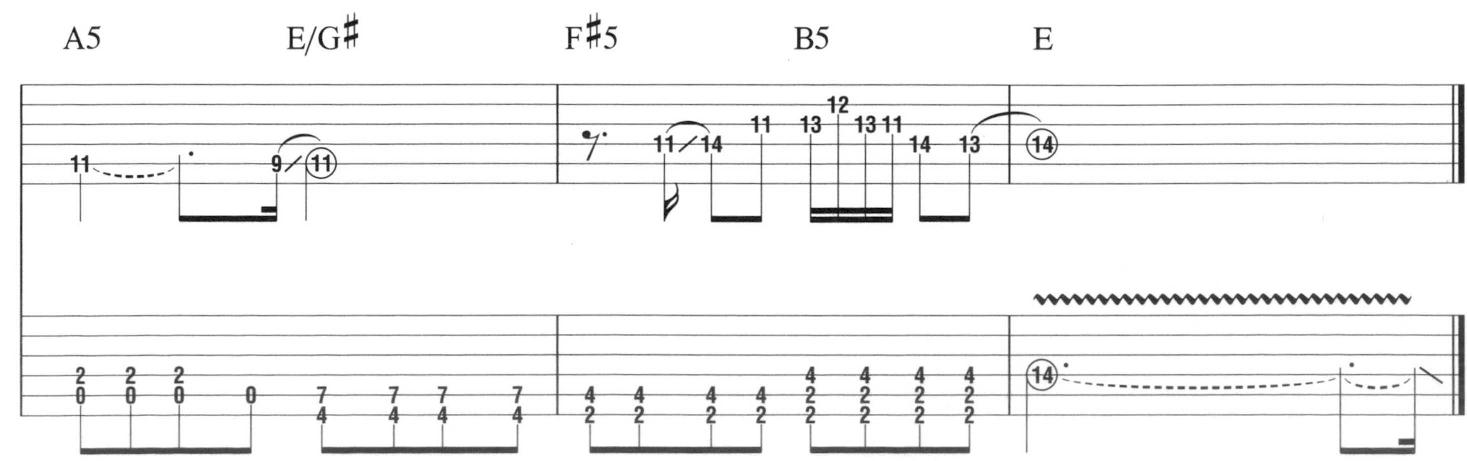

Thank God for Girls

Words and Music by Rivers Cuomo, Alex Goose, Craig Michel Balzer, Bruce Balzer and Bill Petti

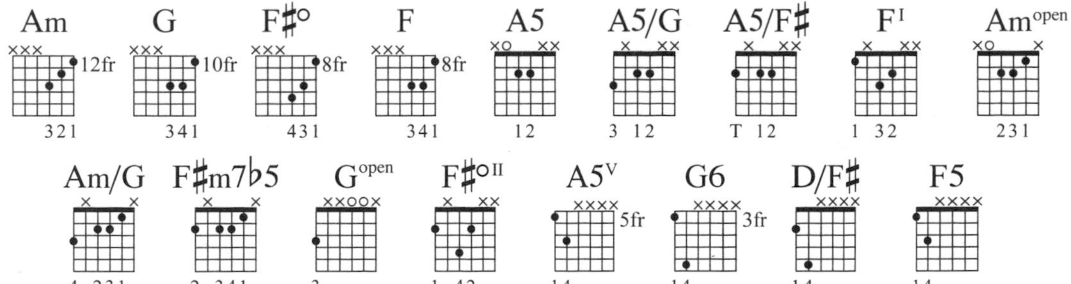

Key of Am

Verse

Moderately slow ♩ = 95

1. The girl in the past - ry shop with the net in her hair is mak-ing a can-no-li for you to take

Am G F♯° F

*Gtr. 1 Rhy. Fig. 1 End Rhy. Fig. 1

*Piano arr. for gtr.

on your hik - ing trip in the woods with your bros that you've known since sec - ond grade. And you

Am G F♯° F

may en-coun-ter dra-gons or ruf-fi-ans and be called up-on to em-ploy your tes - tos - ter-one

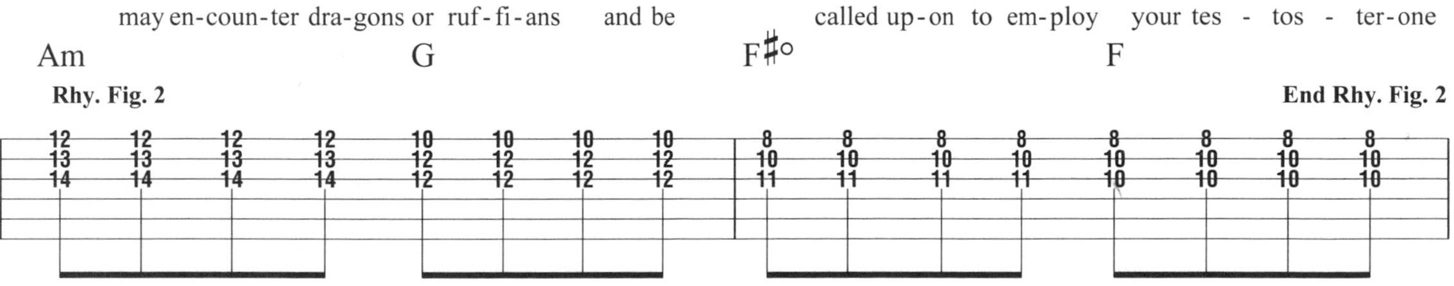

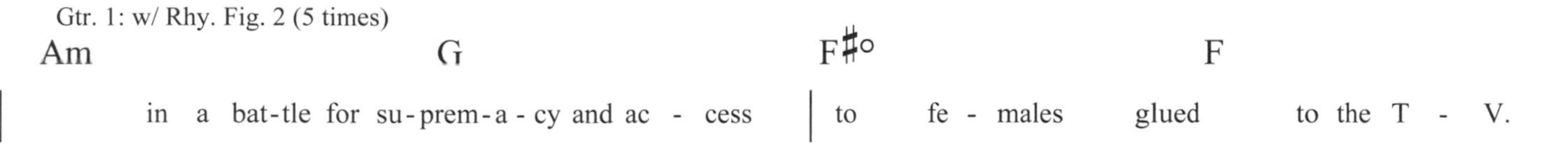

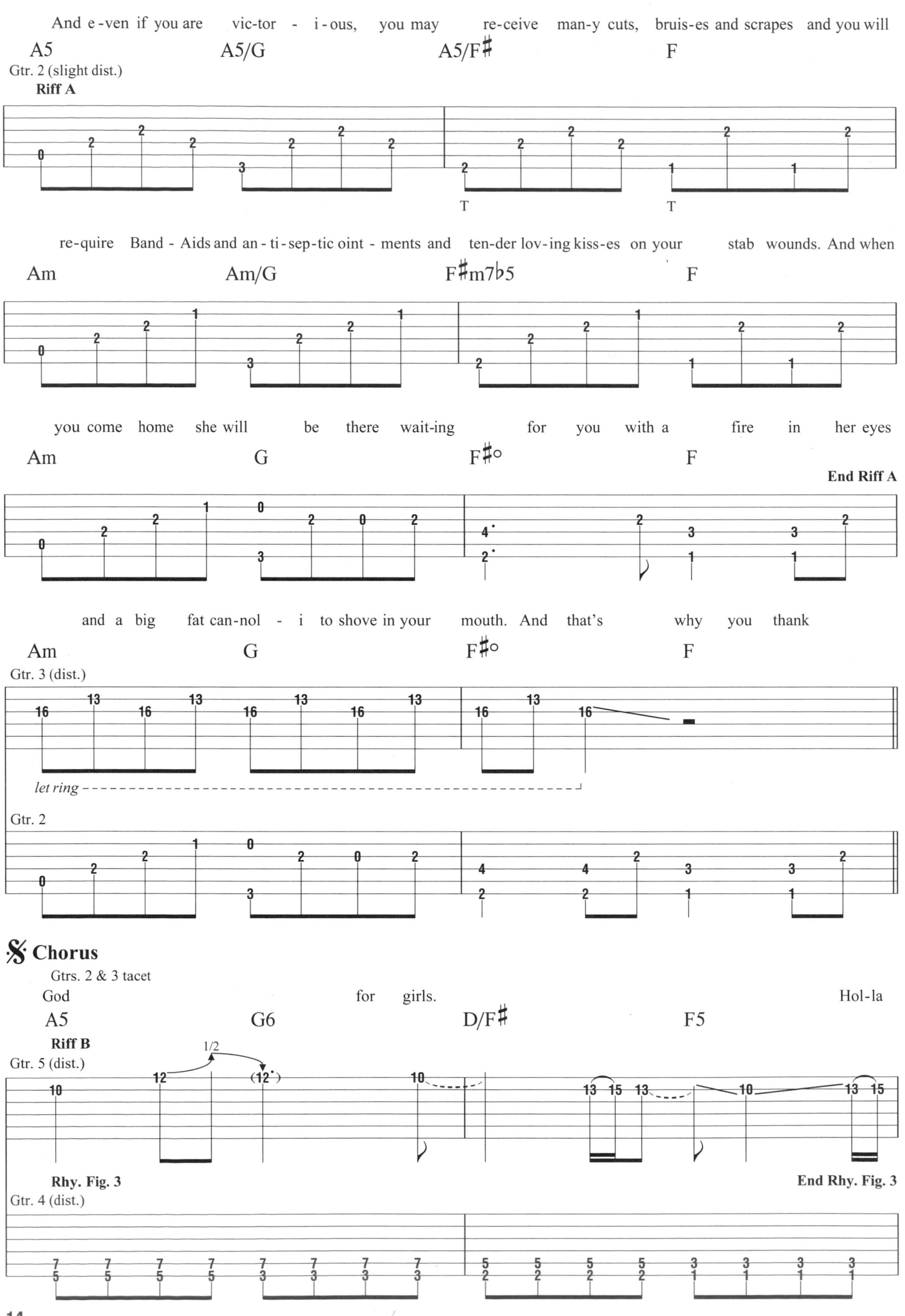
And e-ven if you are vic-tor - i-ous, you may re-ceive man-y cuts, bruis-es and scrapes and you will
A5 A5/G A5/F♯ F
Gtr. 2 (slight dist.)
Riff A
re-quire Band - Aids and an-ti-sep-tic oint - ments and ten-der lov-ing kiss-es on your stab wounds. And when
Am Am/G F♯m7♭5 F
you come home she will be there wait-ing for you with a fire in her eyes
Am G F♯° F
End Riff A
and a big fat can-nol - i to shove in your mouth. And that's why you thank
Am G F♯° F
Gtr. 3 (dist.)
let ring
Gtr. 2
Chorus
Gtrs. 2 & 3 tacet
God for girls. Hol-la
A5 G6 D/F♯ F5
Riff B
Gtr. 5 (dist.)
1/2
Rhy. Fig. 3
End Rhy. Fig. 3
Gtr. 4 (dist.)

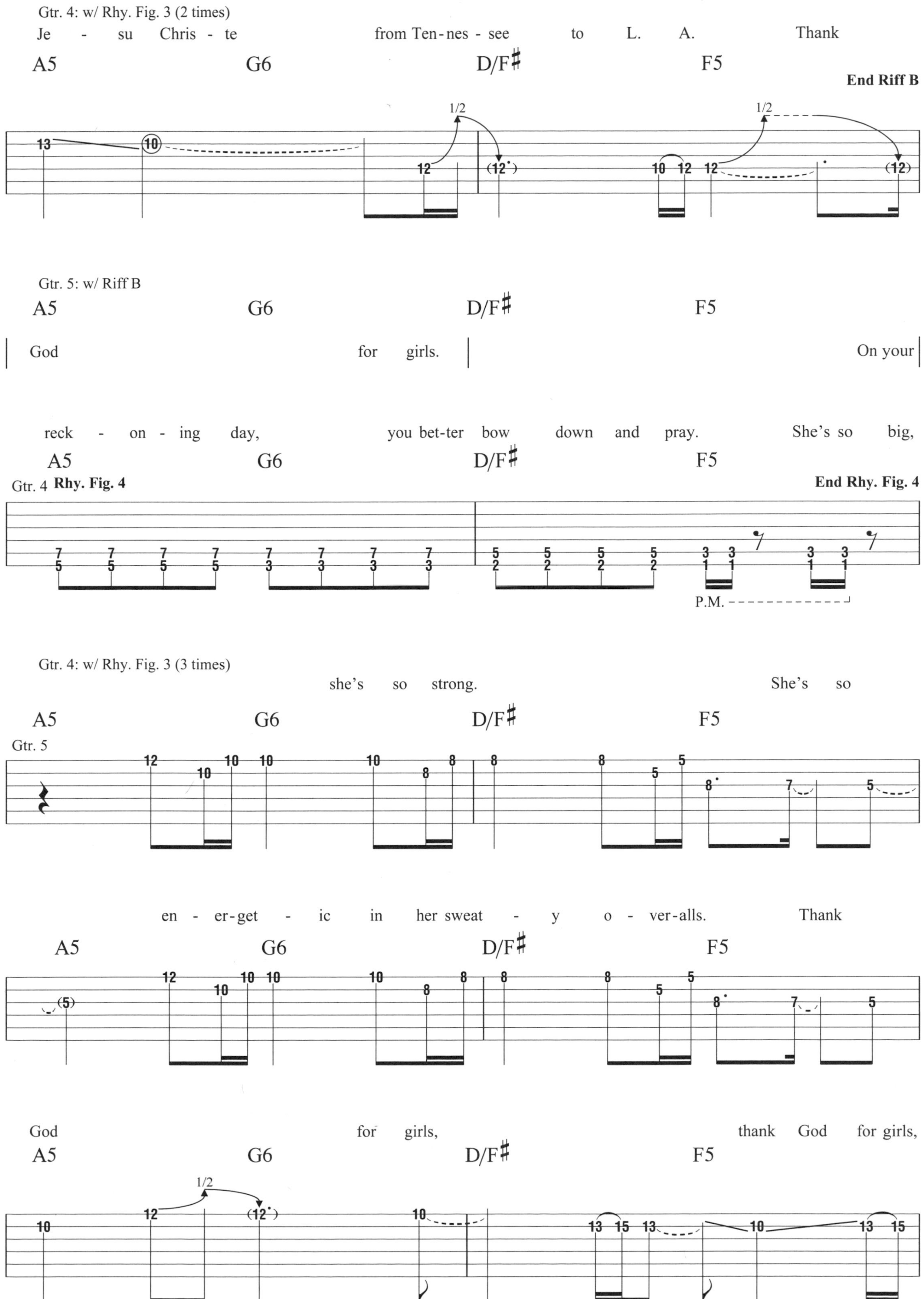
Gtr. 4: w/ Rhy. Fig. 3 (2 times)
Je - su Chris - te from Ten-nes - see to L. A. Thank
A5 G6 D/F♯ F5
End Riff B
Gtr. 5: w/ Riff B
A5 G6 D/F♯ F5
God for girls. On your
reck - on - ing day, you bet-ter bow down and pray. She's so big,
A5 G6 D/F♯ F5
Gtr. 4 Rhy. Fig. 4
End Rhy. Fig. 4
P.M.
Gtr. 4: w/ Rhy. Fig. 3 (3 times)
she's so strong. She's so
A5 G6 D/F♯ F5
Gtr. 5
en - er-get - ic in her sweat - y o - ver-alls. Thank
A5 G6 D/F♯ F5
God for girls, thank God for girls,
A5 G6 D/F♯ F5

To Coda

Gtr. 4: w/ Rhy. Fig. 4

thank God for girls.

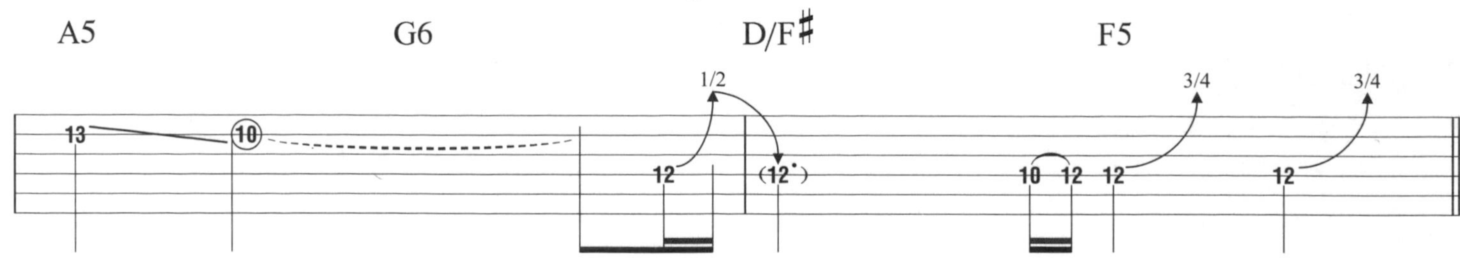

Verse

Gtr. 5 tacet

2. I'm so glad I got a girl to think of e-ven though she is-n't mine.

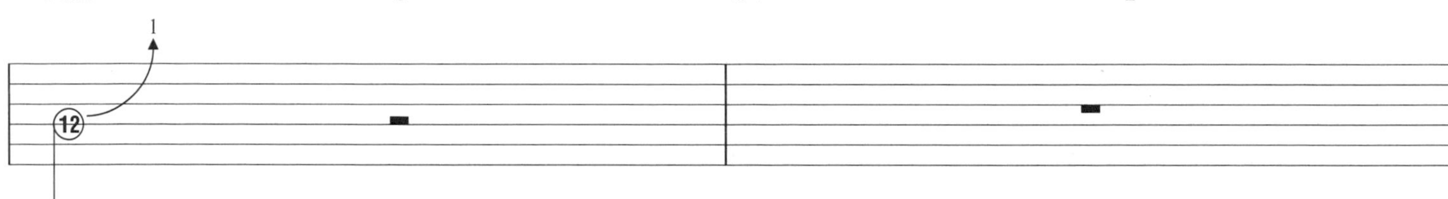

Am G F♯° F

I think a-bout her all the day and all the night. It's e - nough to know that she's a - live. She says I

Gtr. 2: w/ Riff A

A5 A5/G

give her sweat - y palms, she al - most had a heart at - tack.

A5/F♯ F

The truth is that I'm just as scared, I don't know how to act.

Am Am/G

I wish that I could get to know her bet - ter, but meet - ing

F♯m7♭5 F

up in real life would cause the il - lu - sion to shat - ter.

Am G F♯° F

I carved her name in - to all the trees, sang a song down on one knee.

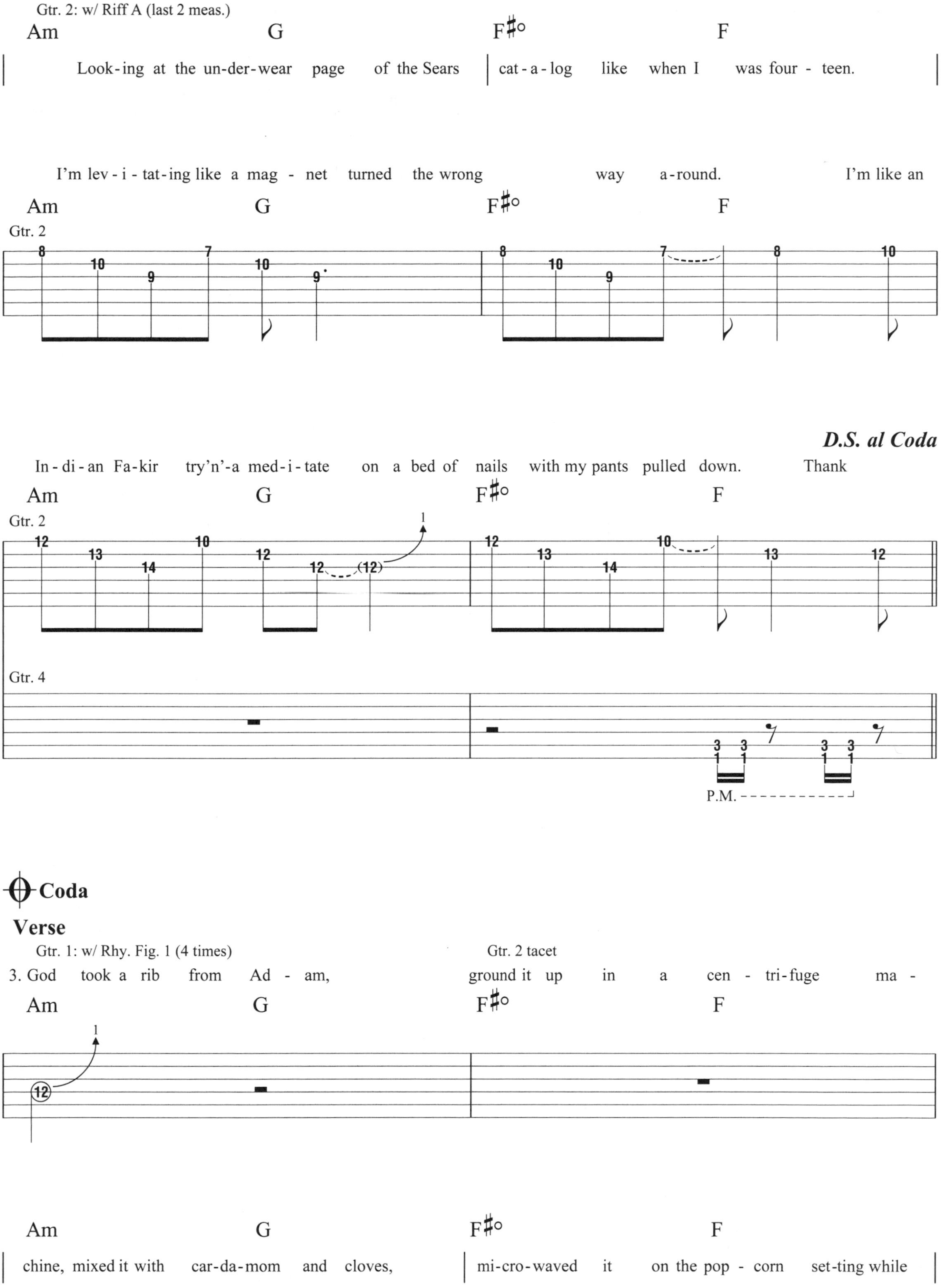

Gtr. 2: w/ Riff A (last 2 meas.)

Am G F♯° F

Look-ing at the un-der-wear page of the Sears cat-a-log like when I was four - teen.

I'm lev-i-tat-ing like a mag - net turned the wrong way a-round. I'm like an

Am G F♯° F

Gtr. 2

D.S. al Coda

In-di-an Fa-kir try'n'-a med-i-tate on a bed of nails with my pants pulled down. Thank

Am G F♯° F

Gtr. 2

Gtr. 4

P.M.

Coda

Verse

Gtr. 1: w/ Rhy. Fig. 1 (4 times)

Gtr. 2 tacet

3. God took a rib from Ad - am, ground it up in a cen - tri-fuge ma -

Am G F♯° F

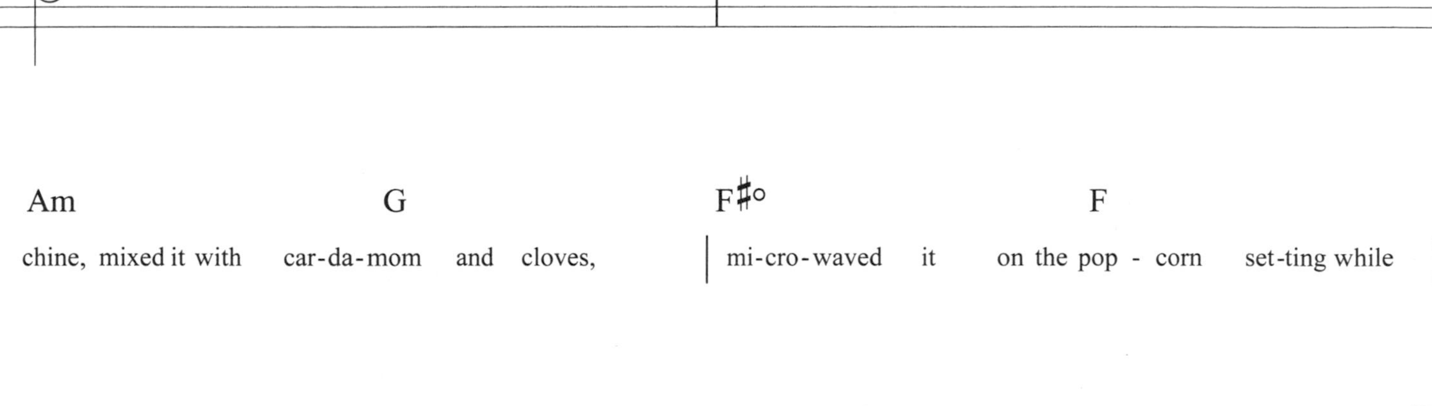

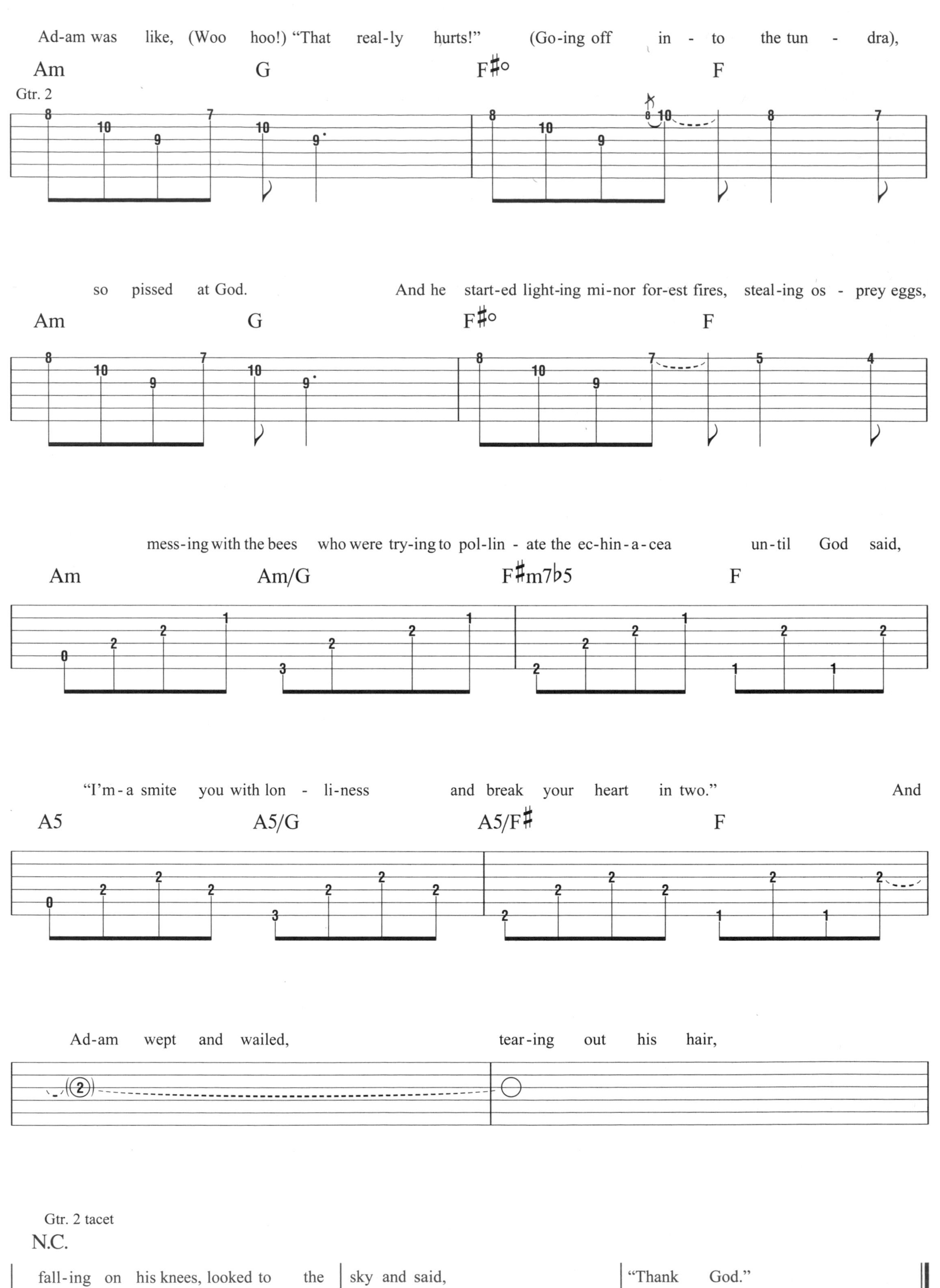
Ad-am was like, (Woo hoo!) "That real-ly hurts!" (Go-ing off in - to the tun - dra),
Am G F♯° F
Gtr. 2
so pissed at God. And he start-ed light-ing mi-nor for-est fires, steal-ing os - prey eggs,
Am G F♯° F
mess-ing with the bees who were try-ing to pol-lin - ate the ec-hin-a-cea un-til God said,
Am Am/G F♯m7♭5 F
"I'm-a smite you with lon - li-ness and break your heart in two." And
A5 A5/G A5/F♯ F
Ad-am wept and wailed, tear-ing out his hair,
Gtr. 2 tacet
N.C.
fall-ing on his knees, looked to the sky and said, "Thank God."

(Girl We Got A) Good Thing

Words and Music by Rivers Cuomo

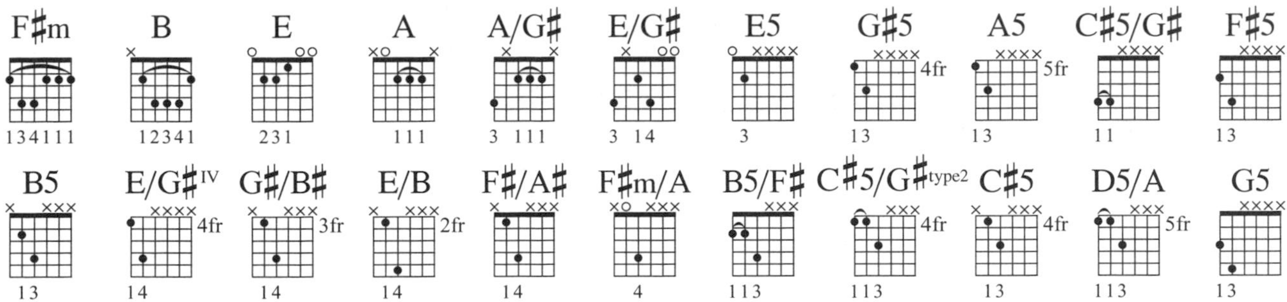

Tune down 1/2 step:
(low to high) E♭-A♭-D♭-G♭-B♭-E♭

Key of E

Intro

Moderately fast ♩ = 130

Girl, we got a

N.C.

Gtr. 1 (elec.)

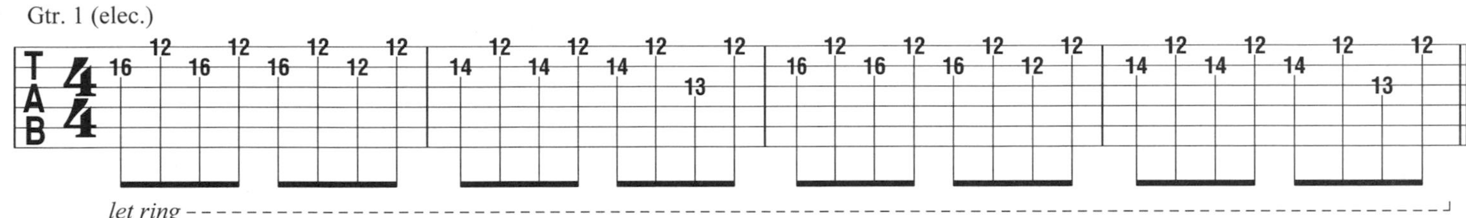

let ring

w/ clean tone

Chorus

F♯m B E A A/G♯

Rhy. Fig. 1 **End Rhy. Fig. 1**

Gtr. 2 (acous.)

good thing. You know where this is head - ing, uh huh. Just a cou-ple

Gtr. 3 (elec.)

Riff A

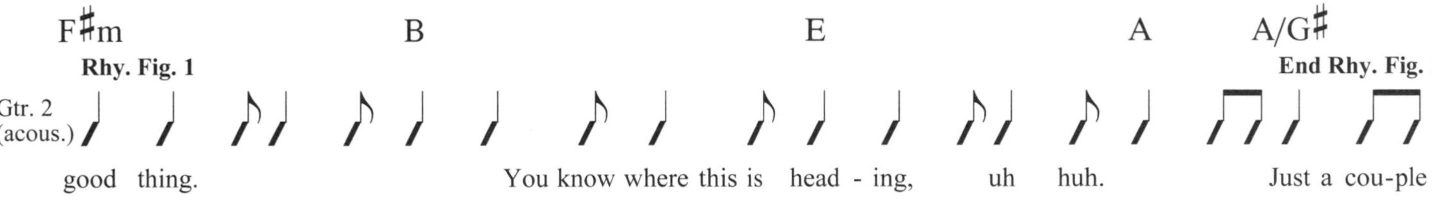

w/ slight dist.

Gtr. 2: w/ Rhy. Fig. 1

love birds hap-py to be sing - ing, uh huh. Girl, we got a

F♯m B E A A/G♯

Gtr. 3

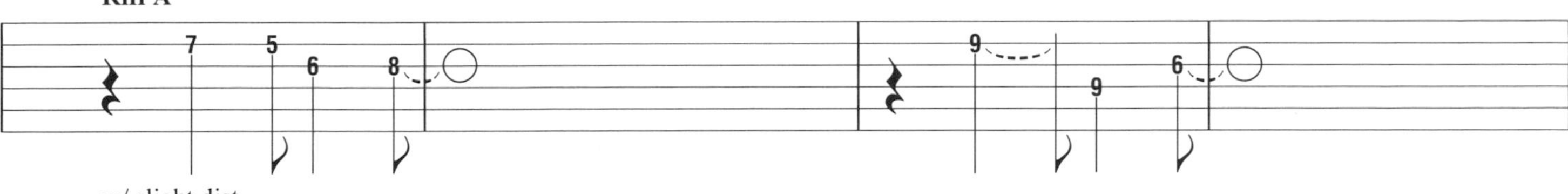

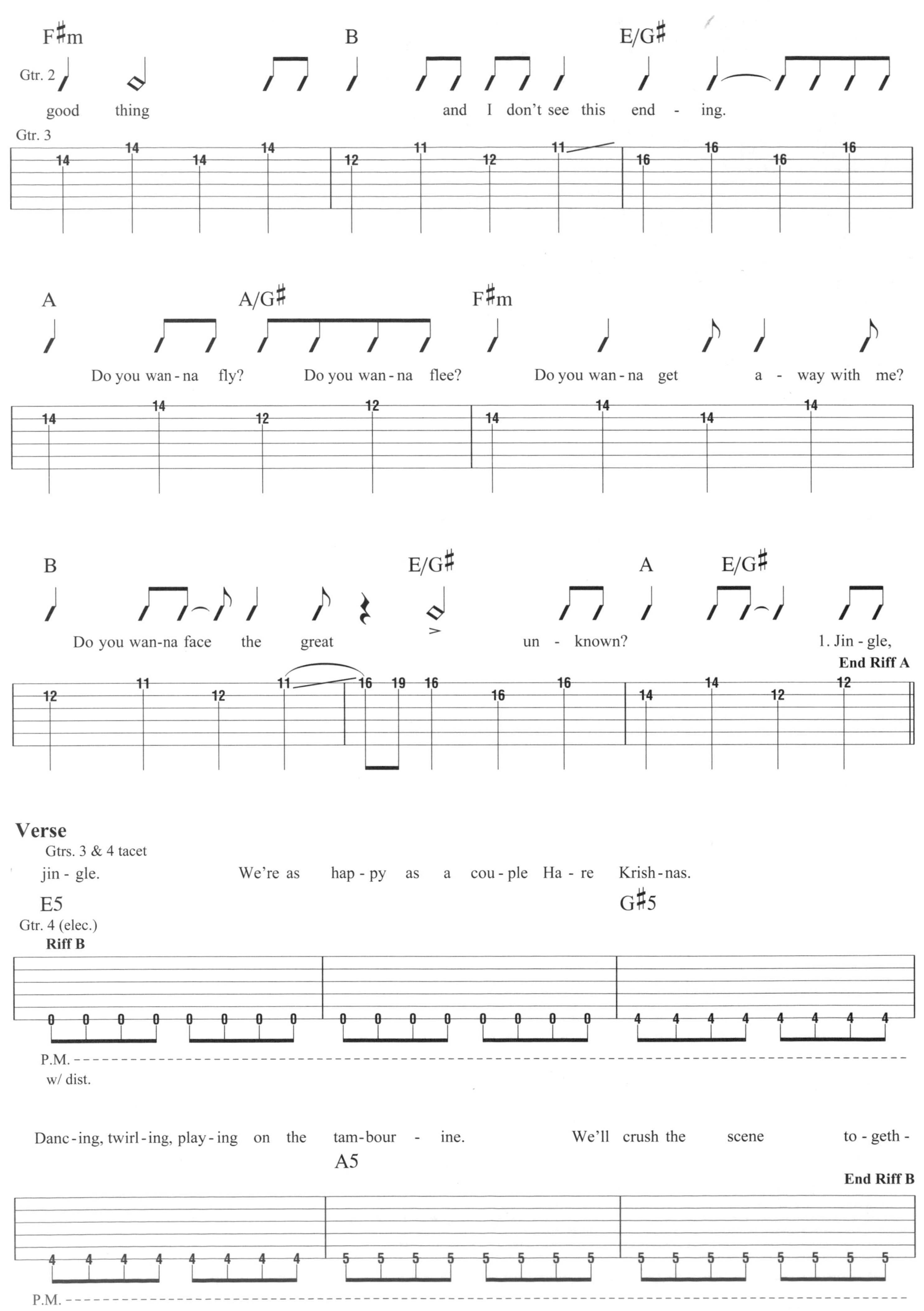
F♯m
B
E/G♯
Gtr. 2
good thing
and I don't see this end - ing.
Gtr. 3
A
A/G♯
F♯m
Do you wan - na fly? Do you wan - na flee? Do you wan - na get a - way with me?
B
E/G♯
A
E/G♯
Do you wan-na face the great un - known? 1. Jin - gle,
End Riff A
Verse
Gtrs. 3 & 4 tacet
jin - gle. We're as hap - py as a cou - ple Ha - re Krish - nas.
E5
G♯5
Gtr. 4 (elec.)
Riff B
P.M.
w/ dist.
Danc - ing, twirl - ing, play - ing on the tam - bour - ine. We'll crush the scene to - geth -
A5
End Riff B
P.M.

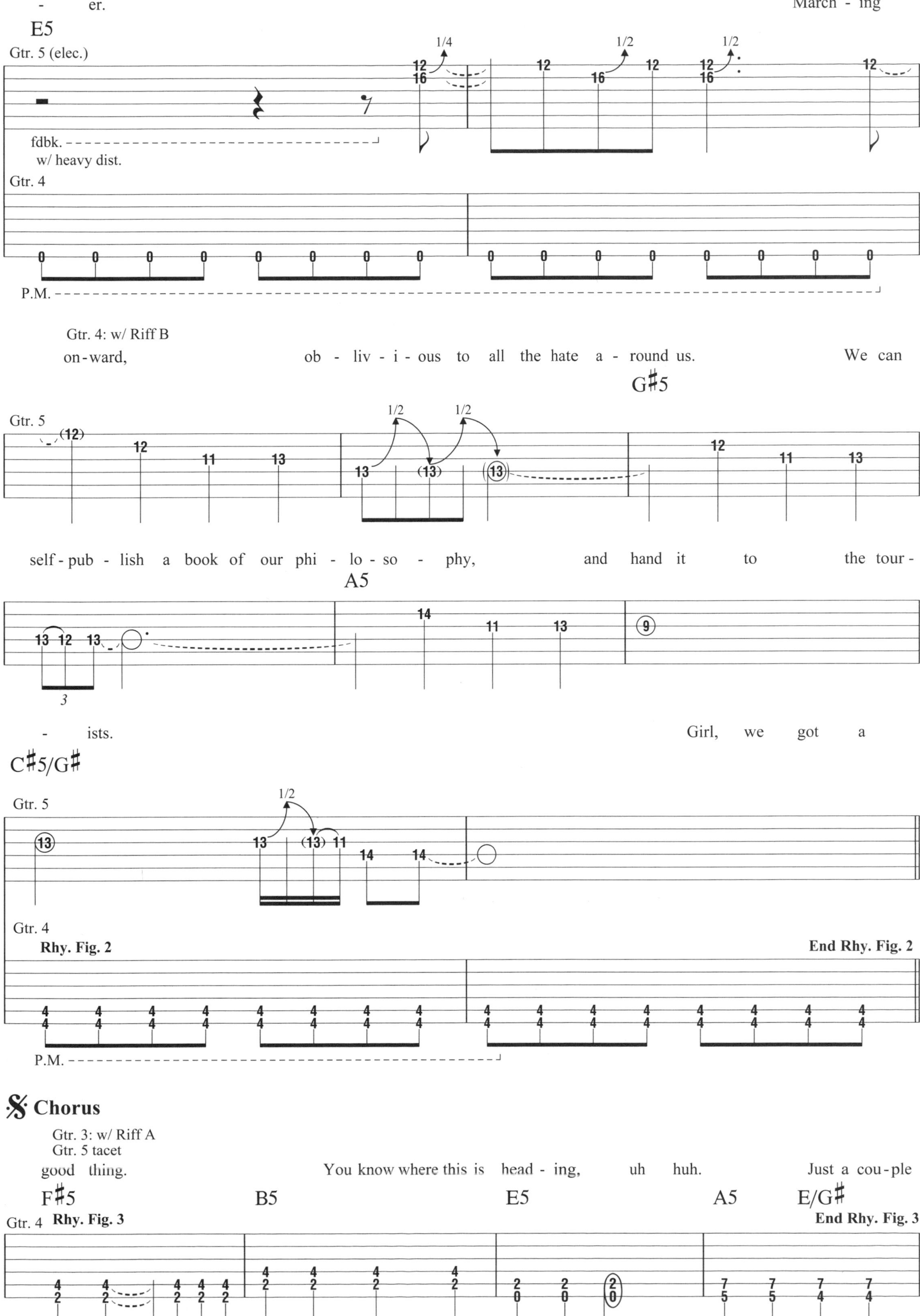
- er.
March - ing
E5
Gtr. 5 (elec.)
fdbk.
w/ heavy dist.
Gtr. 4
P.M.
Gtr. 4: w/ Riff B
on-ward, ob - liv - i - ous to all the hate a - round us. We can
G♯5
Gtr. 5
self-pub - lish a book of our phi - lo - so - phy, and hand it to the tour -
A5
- ists. Girl, we got a
C♯5/G♯
Gtr. 5
Gtr. 4
Rhy. Fig. 2
End Rhy. Fig. 2
P.M.
Chorus
Gtr. 3: w/ Riff A
Gtr. 5 tacet
good thing. You know where this is head - ing, uh huh. Just a cou-ple
F♯5
B5
E5
A5
E/G♯
Gtr. 4 Rhy. Fig. 3
End Rhy. Fig. 3

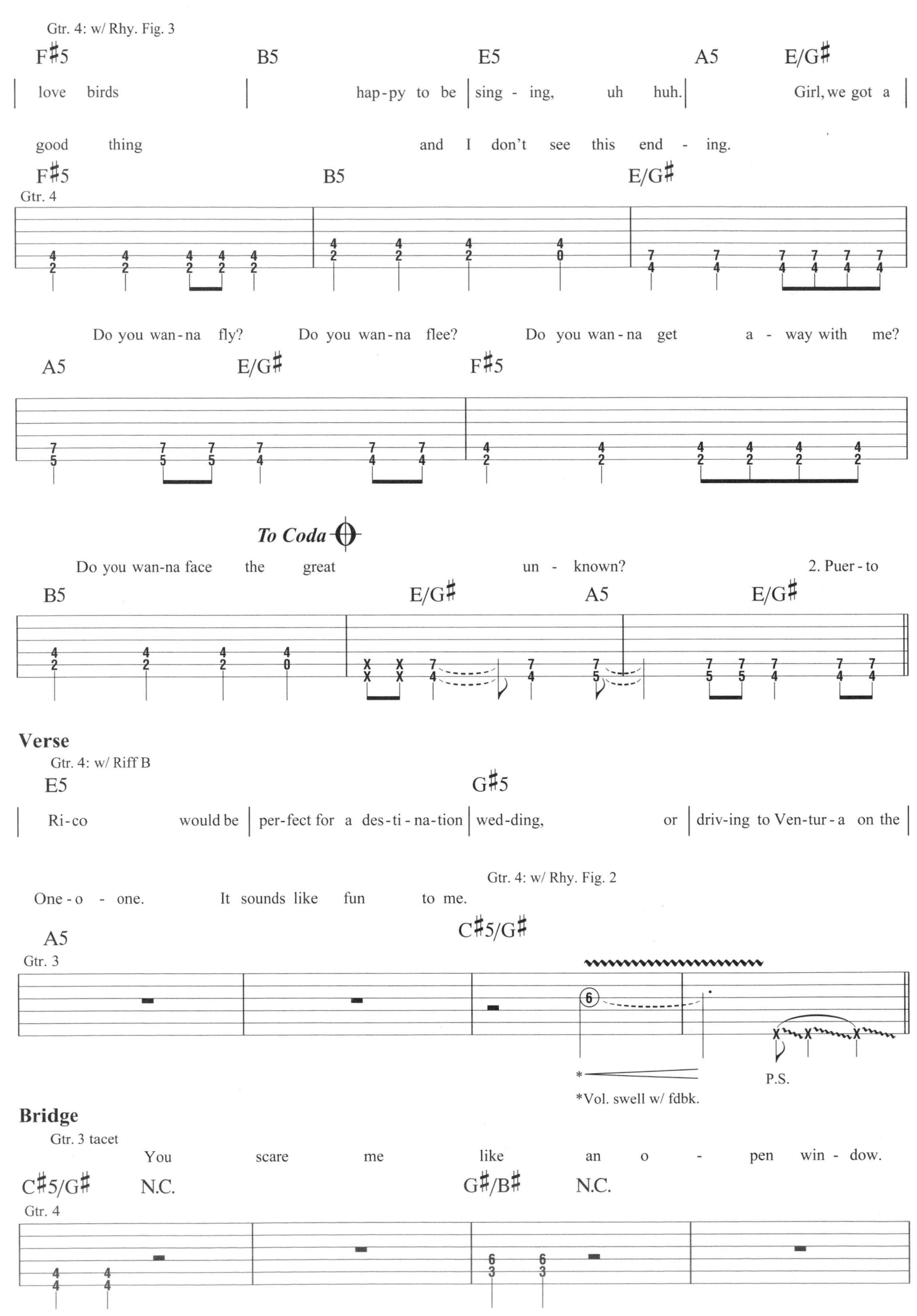
Gtr. 4: w/ Rhy. Fig. 3
F♯5 B5 E5 A5 E/G♯
love birds hap-py to be sing - ing, uh huh. Girl, we got a
good thing and I don't see this end - ing.
F♯5 B5 E/G♯
Gtr. 4
Do you wan-na fly? Do you wan-na flee? Do you wan-na get a - way with me?
A5 E/G♯ F♯5
To Coda
Do you wan-na face the great un - known? 2. Puer-to
B5 E/G♯ A5 E/G♯
Verse
Gtr. 4: w/ Riff B
E5 G♯5
Ri-co would be per-fect for a des-ti-na-tion wed-ding, or driv-ing to Ven-tur-a on the
One-o - one. It sounds like fun to me.
Gtr. 4: w/ Rhy. Fig. 2
A5 C♯5/G♯
Gtr. 3
P.S.
*Vol. swell w/ fdbk.
Bridge
Gtr. 3 tacet
You scare me like an o - pen win - dow.
C♯5/G♯ N.C. G♯/B♯ N.C.
Gtr. 4

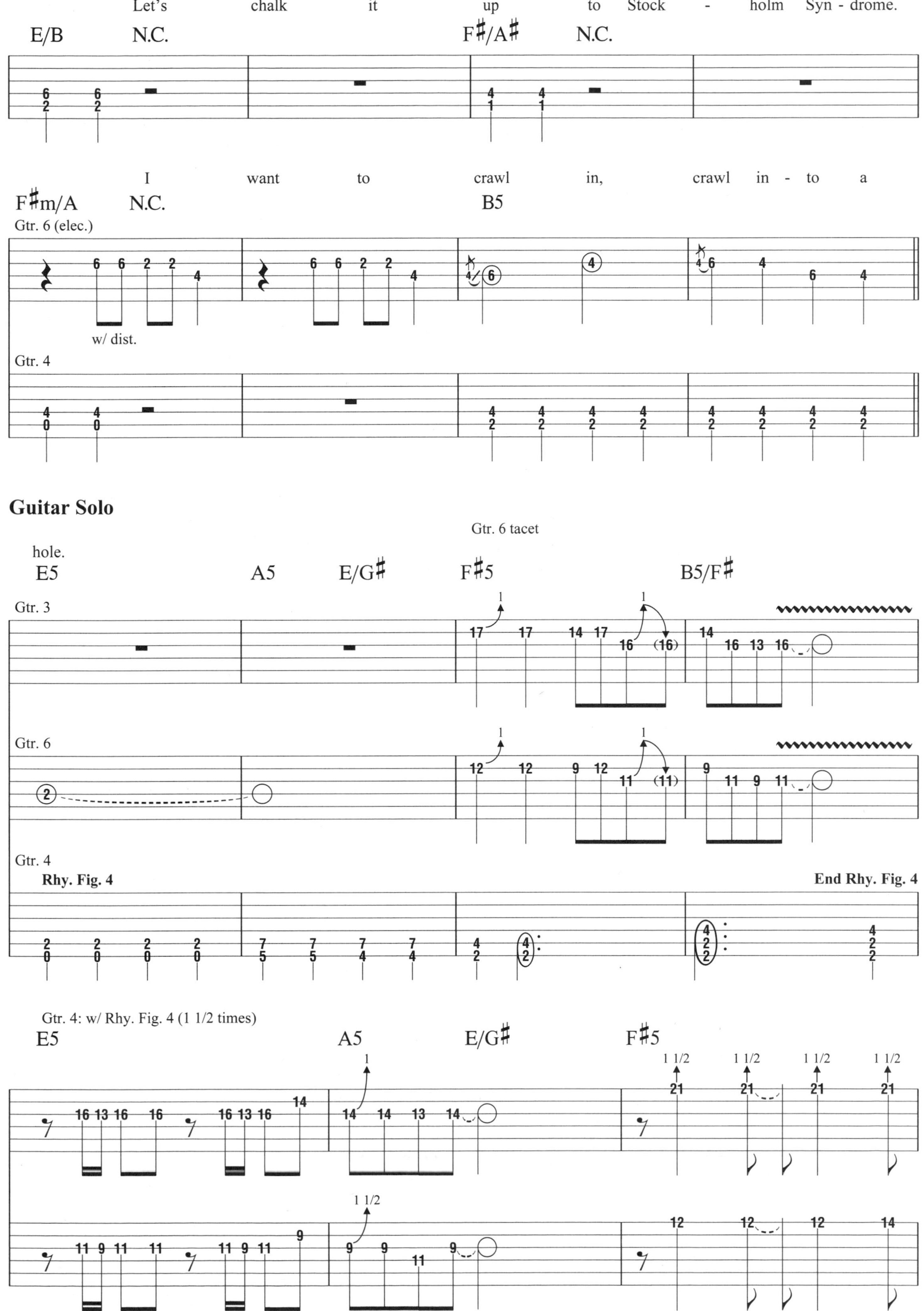
Let's chalk it up to Stock - holm Syn - drome.
E/B
N.C.
F♯/A♯
N.C.
I want to crawl in, crawl in - to a
F♯m/A
N.C.
B5
Gtr. 6 (elec.)
w/ dist.
Gtr. 4
Guitar Solo
Gtr. 6 tacet
hole.
E5
A5
E/G♯
F♯5
B5/F♯
Gtr. 3
Gtr. 6
Gtr. 4
Rhy. Fig. 4
End Rhy. Fig. 4
Gtr. 4: w/ Rhy. Fig. 4 (1 1/2 times)
E5
A5
E/G♯
F♯5

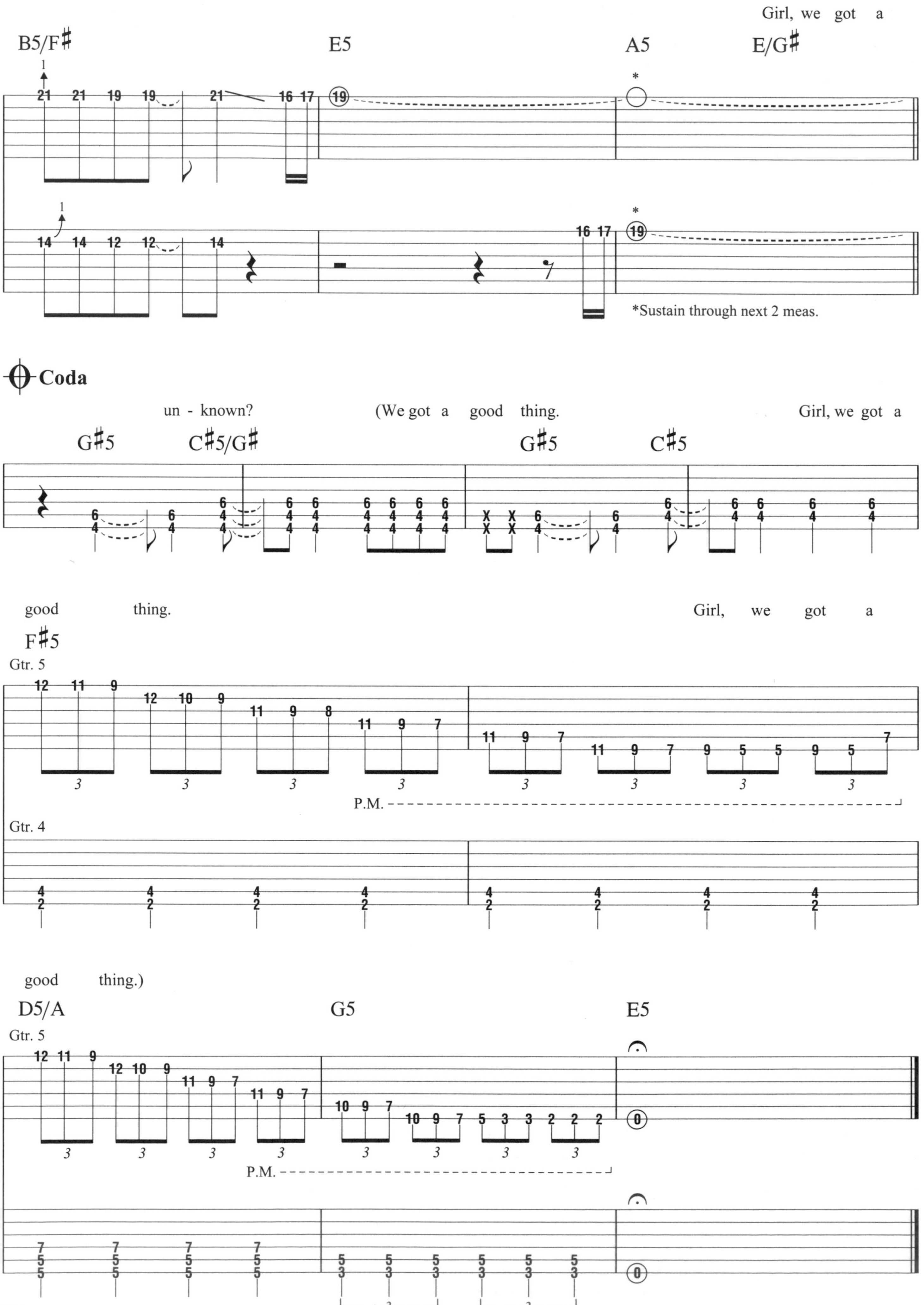
D.S. al Coda
Girl, we got a
B5/F♯
E5
A5
E/G♯
*Sustain through next 2 meas.
Coda
un - known?
(We got a good thing.
Girl, we got a
G♯5
C♯5/G♯
G♯5
C♯5
good thing.
Girl, we got a
F♯5
Gtr. 5
P.M.
Gtr. 4
good thing.)
D5/A
G5
E5
Gtr. 5
P.M.

Do You Wanna Get High?

Words and Music by Rivers Cuomo

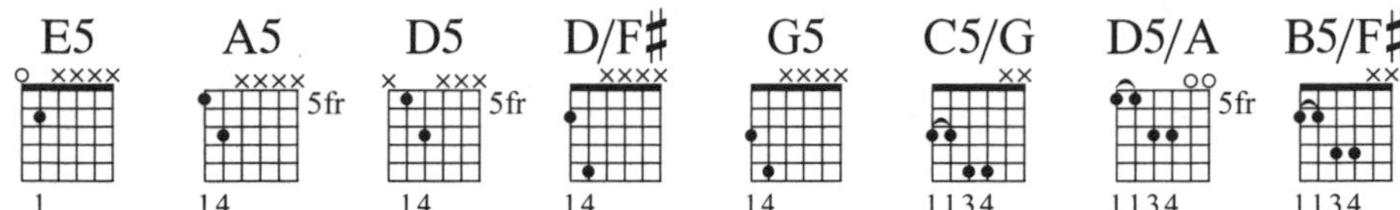

Tune down 1/2 step:
(low to high) E♭-A♭-D♭-G♭-B♭-E♭

Key of E minor

Verse

Moderately fast ♩ = 132

1. Crush up the blue and in-hale through your nose. Scrape

E5 A5 D5 D/F♯ G5 D/F♯

Gtrs. 1 & 2 (dist.)

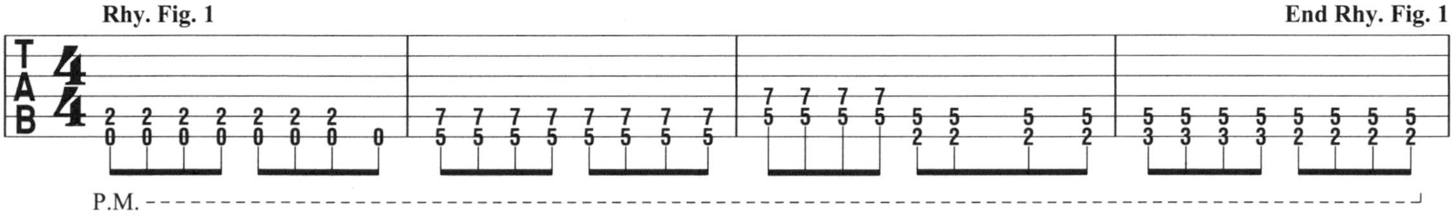

Rhy. Fig. 1 **End Rhy. Fig. 1**

P.M.

Gtrs. 1 & 2: w/ Rhy. Fig. 1

E5 A5 D5 D/F♯ G5 D/F♯

ev-'ry quark | from the wood | in the floor. | She said, ||

Chorus

Half-time feel

Gtrs. 1 & 2: w/ Rhy. Fig. 1 (4 times)

E5 A5 D5 D/F♯ G5 D/F♯

| "Do you wan-na get high? | Don't eat no din-ner to-night. | |

E5 A5 D5 D/F♯ G5 D/F♯

| I took a road trip to Mex - i - co and scored | a hun - dred count. | |

E5 A5 D5 D/F♯ G5 D/F♯

| Do you wan-na get high? | It's like we're fall-ing in love. | |

E5 A5 D5 D/F♯ G5 D/F♯

| We can lis-ten to Bach - a-rach and stop | at an - y point." | 2. Now our bones ||

Verse

Gtrs. 1 & 2: w/ Rhy. Fig. 1 (2 times)

E5 A5 D5 D/F♯ G5 D/F♯

| start to ache | as we cramp | on the pot | and we fall |

E5 A5 D5 D/F♯ G5 D/F♯

| to the floor | with our face | in a knot. | She said, ||

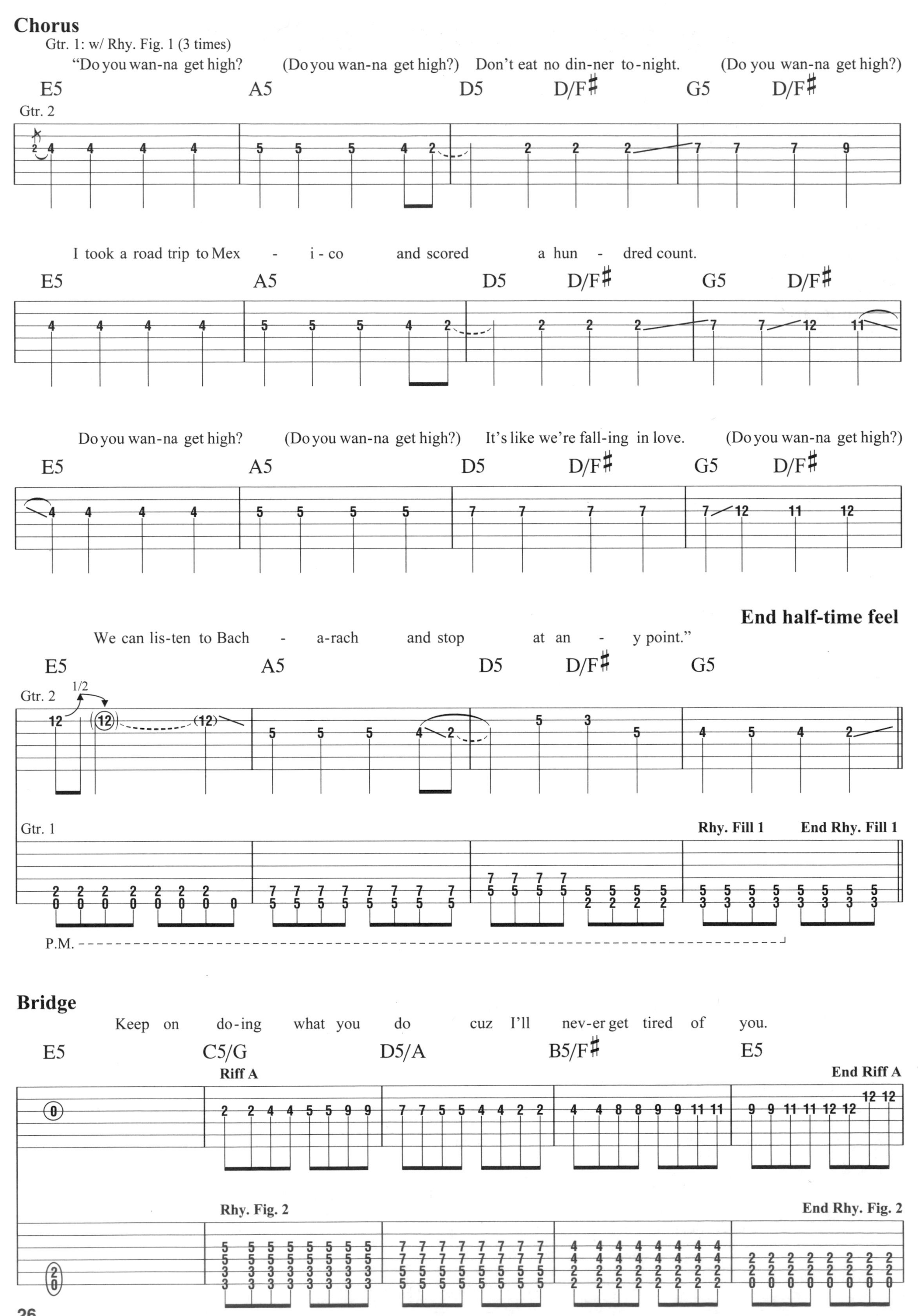
Chorus
Gtr. 1: w/ Rhy. Fig. 1 (3 times)
"Do you wan-na get high? (Do you wan-na get high?) Don't eat no din-ner to-night. (Do you wan-na get high?)
E5 A5 D5 D/F♯ G5 D/F♯
Gtr. 2
I took a road trip to Mex - i - co and scored a hun - dred count.
E5 A5 D5 D/F♯ G5 D/F♯
Do you wan-na get high? (Do you wan-na get high?) It's like we're fall-ing in love. (Do you wan-na get high?)
E5 A5 D5 D/F♯ G5 D/F♯
End half-time feel
We can lis-ten to Bach - a-rach and stop at an - y point."
E5 A5 D5 D/F♯ G5
Gtr. 2
1/2
Gtr. 1
Rhy. Fill 1
End Rhy. Fill 1
P.M.
Bridge
Keep on do-ing what you do cuz I'll nev-er get tired of you.
E5 C5/G D5/A B5/F♯ E5
Riff A
End Riff A
Rhy. Fig. 2
End Rhy. Fig. 2

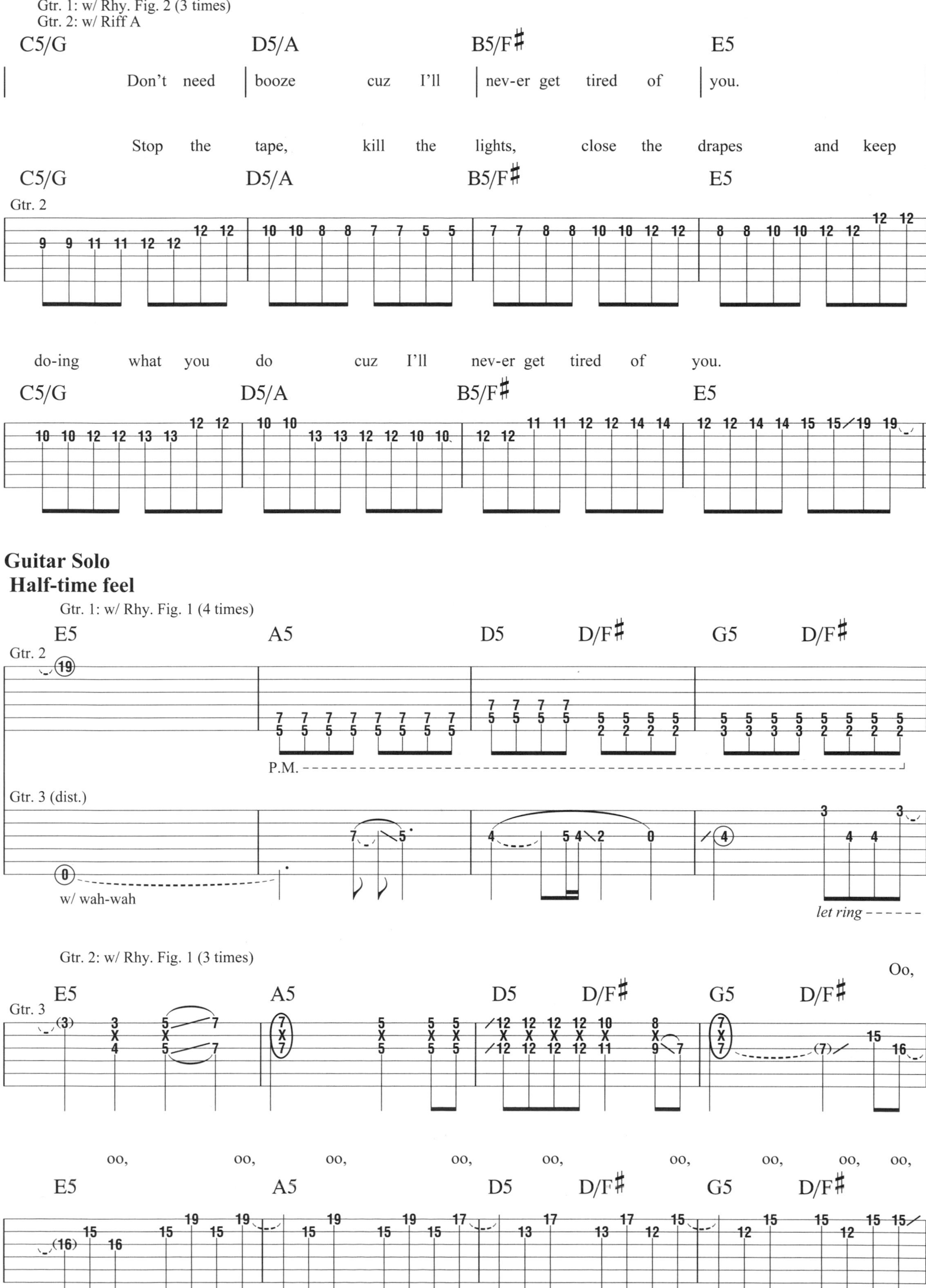

Gtr. 1: w/ Rhy. Fig. 2 (3 times)
Gtr. 2: w/ Riff A
C5/G
D5/A
B5/F♯
E5
Don't need booze cuz I'll nev-er get tired of you.
Stop the tape, kill the lights, close the drapes and keep
Gtr. 2
do-ing what you do cuz I'll nev-er get tired of you.
Guitar Solo
Half-time feel
Gtr. 1: w/ Rhy. Fig. 1 (4 times)
A5
D5
D/F♯
G5
P.M.
Gtr. 3 (dist.)
w/ wah-wah
let ring
Gtr. 2: w/ Rhy. Fig. 1 (3 times)
Gtr. 3
Oo,
oo, oo, oo, oo, oo, oo, oo, oo, oo,

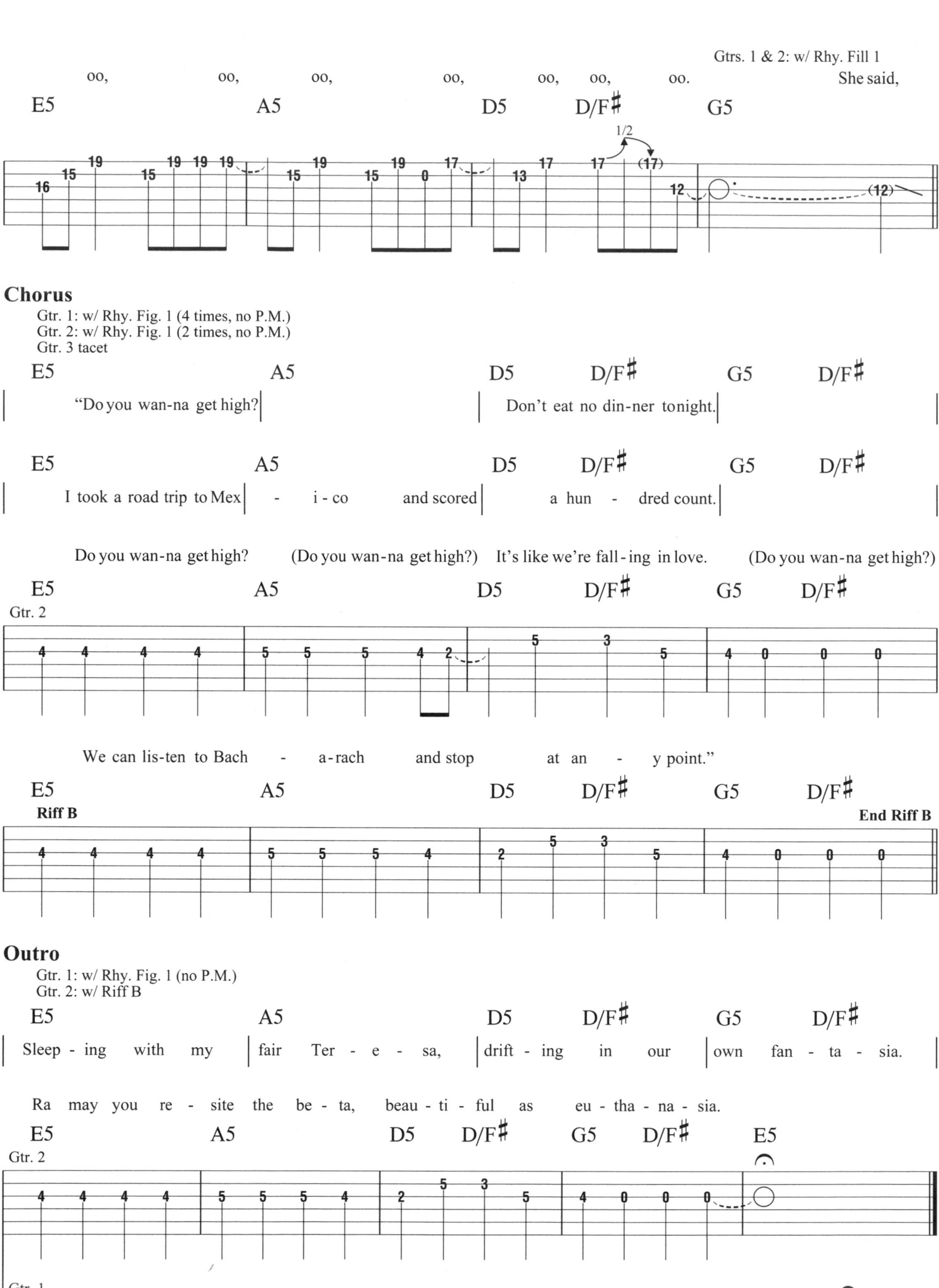
Gtrs. 1 & 2: w/ Rhy. Fill 1
oo, oo, oo, oo, oo, oo, oo. She said,
E5 A5 D5 D/F♯ G5
1/2
Chorus
Gtr. 1: w/ Rhy. Fig. 1 (4 times, no P.M.)
Gtr. 2: w/ Rhy. Fig. 1 (2 times, no P.M.)
Gtr. 3 tacet
E5 A5 D5 D/F♯ G5 D/F♯
"Do you wan-na get high? Don't eat no din-ner tonight.
E5 A5 D5 D/F♯ G5 D/F♯
I took a road trip to Mex - i - co and scored a hun - dred count.
Do you wan-na get high? (Do you wan-na get high?) It's like we're fall-ing in love. (Do you wan-na get high?)
E5 A5 D5 D/F♯ G5 D/F♯
Gtr. 2
We can lis-ten to Bach - a-rach and stop at an - y point."
E5 A5 D5 D/F♯ G5 D/F♯
Riff B
End Riff B
Outro
Gtr. 1: w/ Rhy. Fig. 1 (no P.M.)
Gtr. 2: w/ Riff B
E5 A5 D5 D/F♯ G5 D/F♯
Sleep - ing with my fair Ter - e - sa, drift - ing in our own fan - ta - sia.
Ra may you re - site the be - ta, beau - ti - ful as eu - tha - na - sia.
E5 A5 D5 D/F♯ G5 D/F♯ E5
Gtr. 2
Gtr. 1

King of the World

Words and Music by Rivers Cuomo and Jarrad Kritzstein

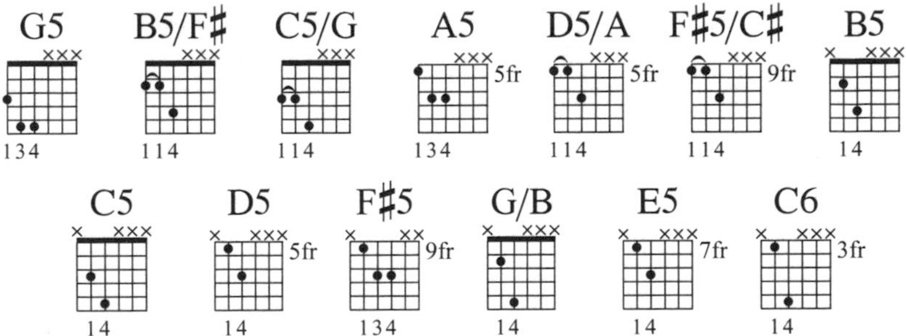

Tune down 1/2 step:
(low to high) E♭-A♭-D♭-G♭-B♭-E♭

Key of G

Intro
Moderately slow ♩ = 84

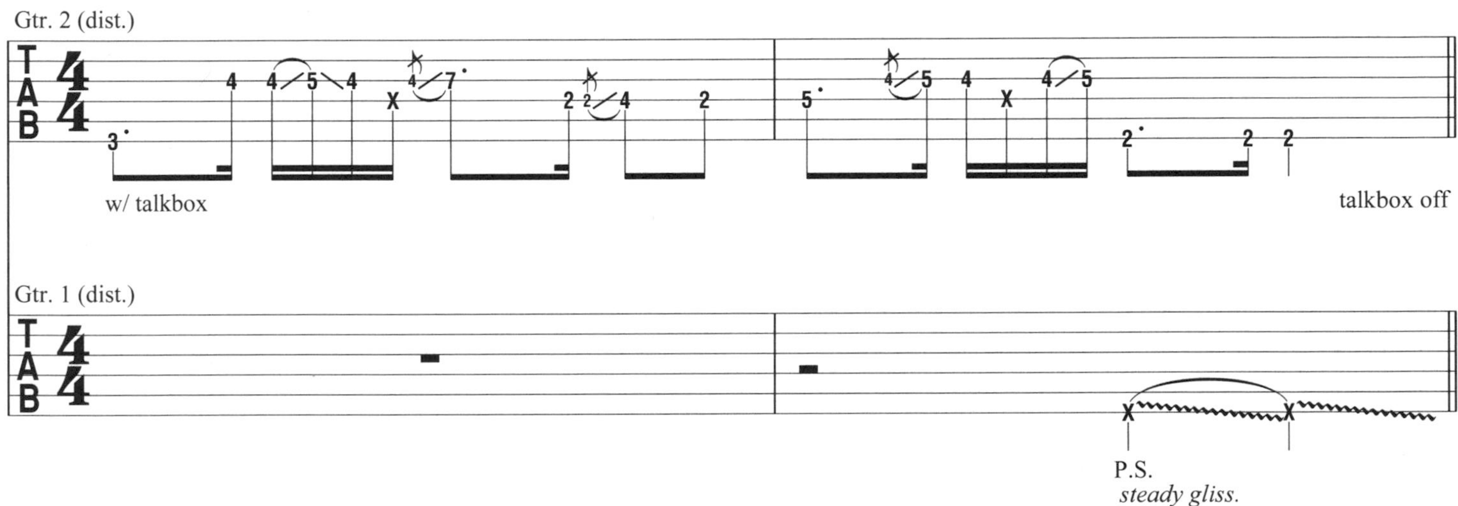

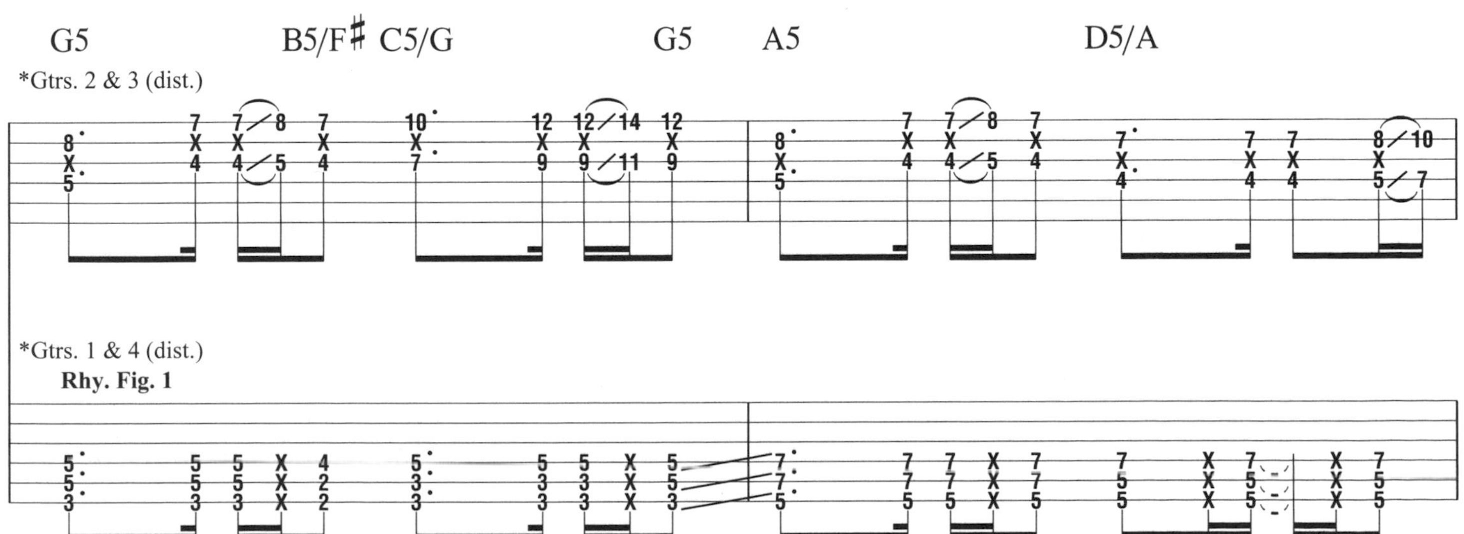

*Composite arrangement; Gtr. 4 doubled throughout.

1. You

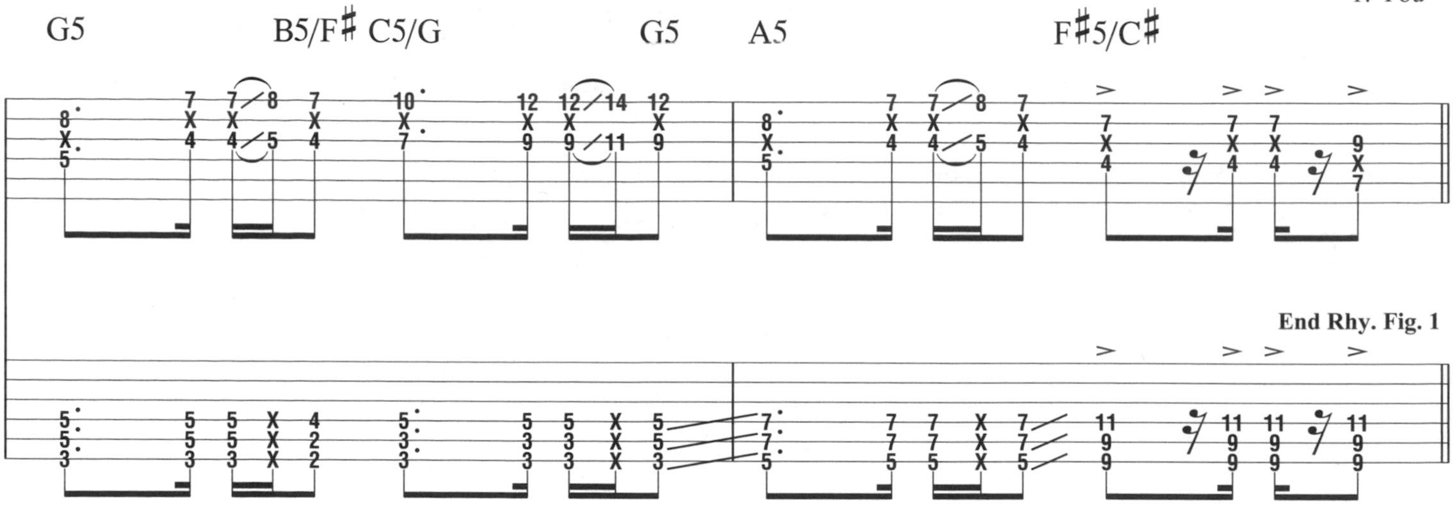
G5
B5/F♯ C5/G
G5
A5
F♯5/C♯
End Rhy. Fig. 1

Verse

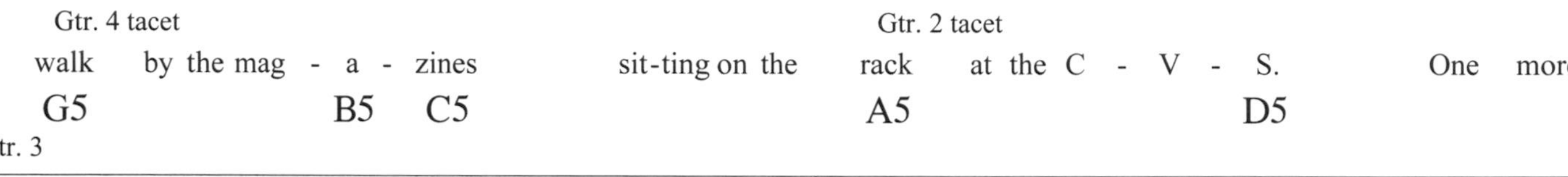
Gtr. 4 tacet
Gtr. 2 tacet
walk by the mag - a - zines sit-ting on the rack at the C - V - S. One more
G5 B5 C5 A5 D5

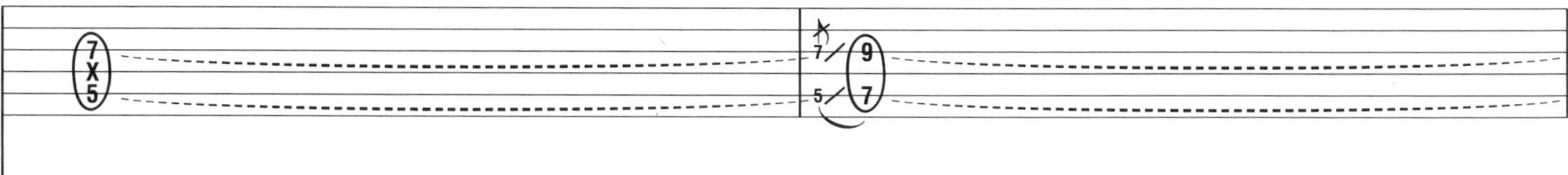
Gtr. 3

Gtr. 2

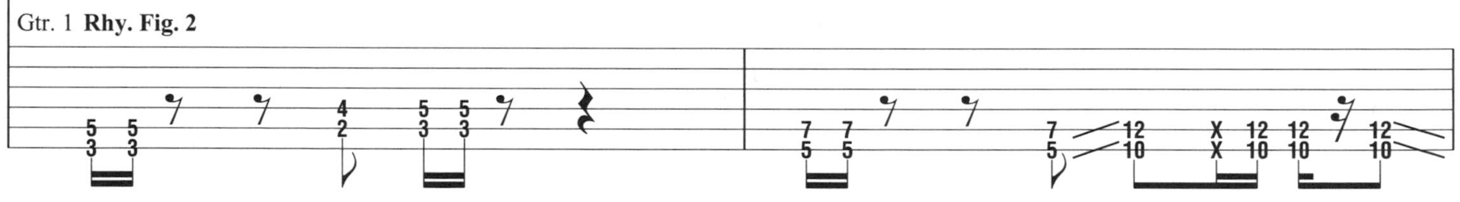
Gtr. 1 Rhy. Fig. 2

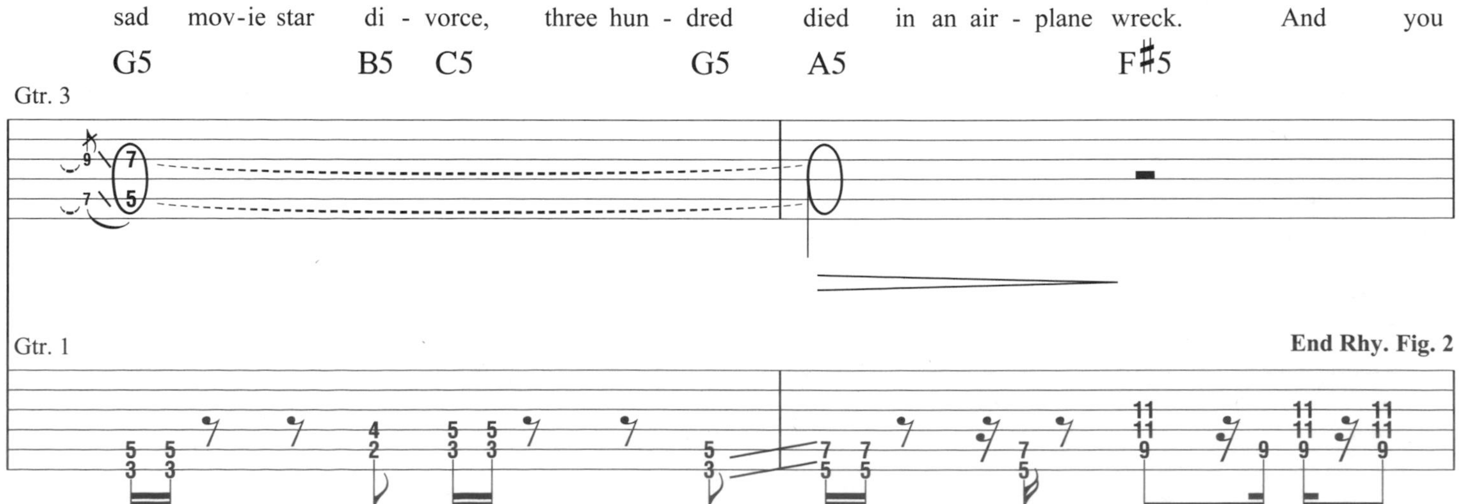
sad mov-ie star di - vorce, three hun - dred died in an air - plane wreck. And you
G5 B5 C5 G5 A5 F♯5
Gtr. 3
Gtr. 1
End Rhy. Fig. 2

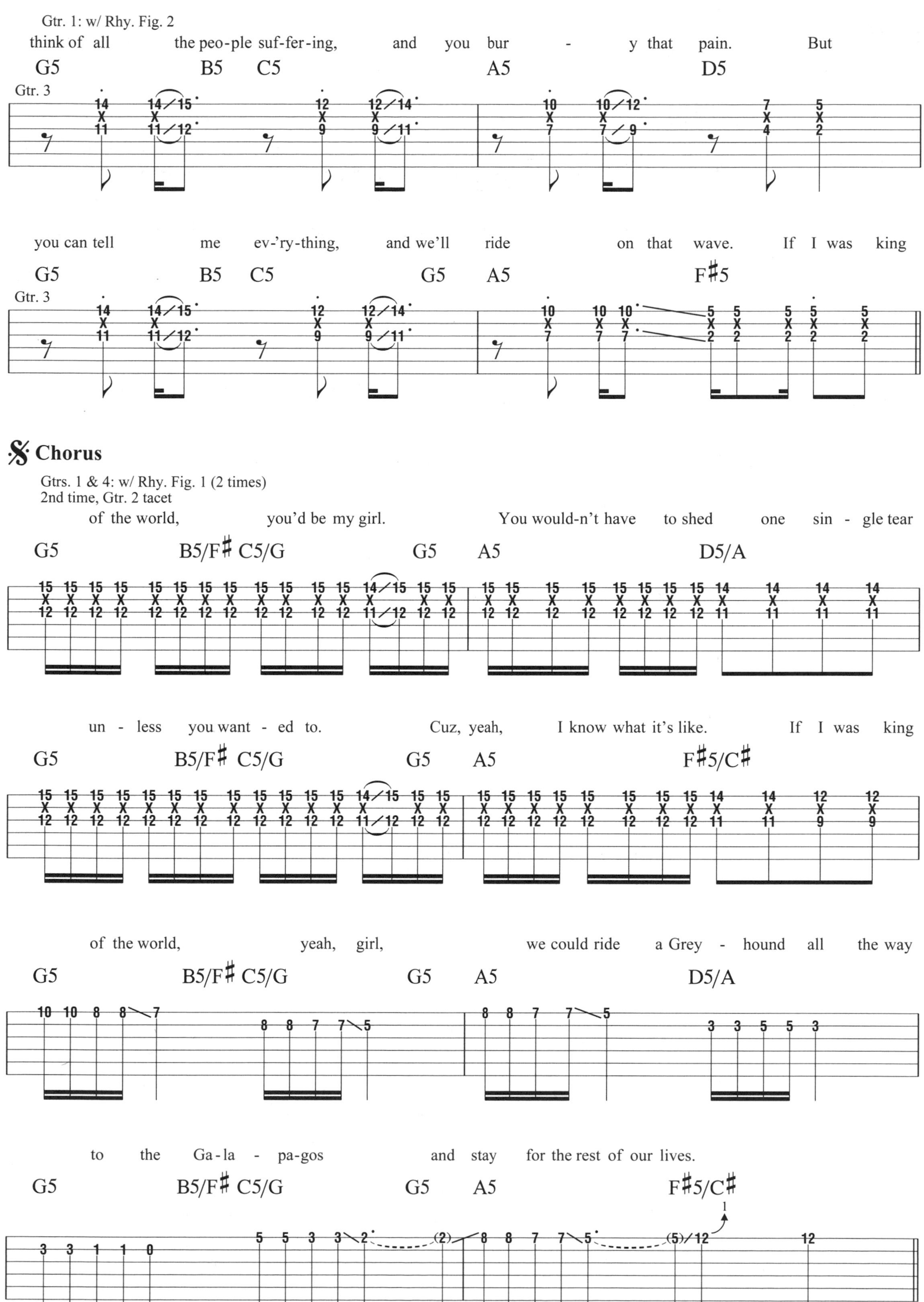

Gtr. 1: w/ Rhy. Fig. 2
think of all the peo-ple suf-fer-ing, and you bur - y that pain. But
G5 B5 C5 A5 D5
Gtr. 3
you can tell me ev-'ry-thing, and we'll ride on that wave. If I was king
G5 B5 C5 G5 A5 F♯5
Gtr. 3
Chorus
Gtrs. 1 & 4: w/ Rhy. Fig. 1 (2 times)
2nd time, Gtr. 2 tacet
of the world, you'd be my girl. You would-n't have to shed one sin - gle tear
G5 B5/F♯ C5/G G5 A5 D5/A
un - less you want - ed to. Cuz, yeah, I know what it's like. If I was king
G5 B5/F♯ C5/G G5 A5 F♯5/C♯
of the world, yeah, girl, we could ride a Grey - hound all the way
G5 B5/F♯ C5/G G5 A5 D5/A
to the Ga-la - pa-gos and stay for the rest of our lives.
G5 B5/F♯ C5/G G5 A5 F♯5/C♯

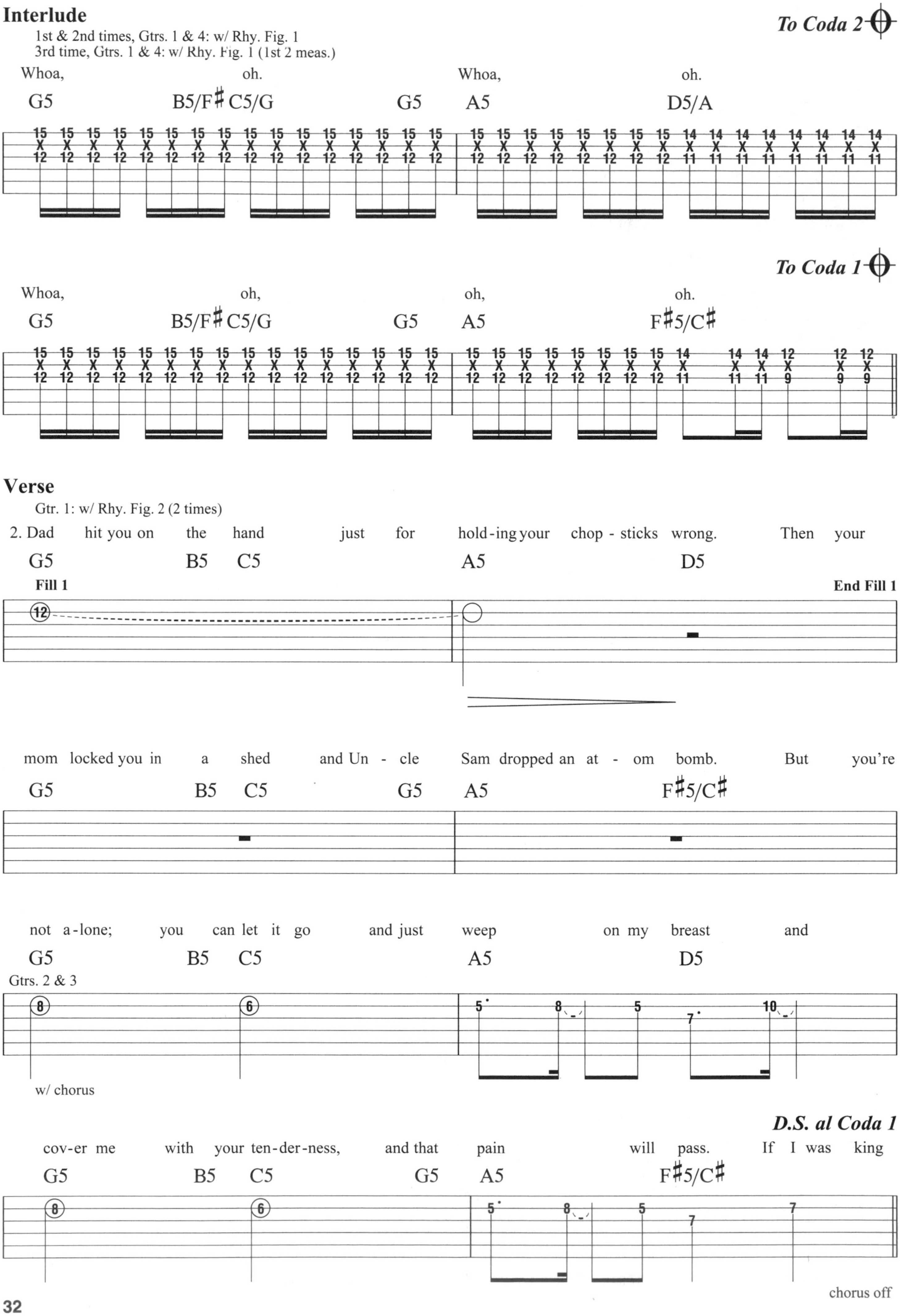

Interlude

To Coda 2 𝄌

1st & 2nd times, Gtrs. 1 & 4: w/ Rhy. Fig. 1
3rd time, Gtrs. 1 & 4: w/ Rhy. Fig. 1 (1st 2 meas.)

Whoa, oh. Whoa, oh.

G5 B5/F♯ C5/G G5 A5 D5/A

To Coda 1 𝄌

Whoa, oh, oh, oh.

G5 B5/F♯ C5/G G5 A5 F♯5/C♯

Verse

Gtr. 1: w/ Rhy. Fig. 2 (2 times)

2. Dad hit you on the hand just for hold-ing your chop - sticks wrong. Then your

G5 B5 C5 A5 D5

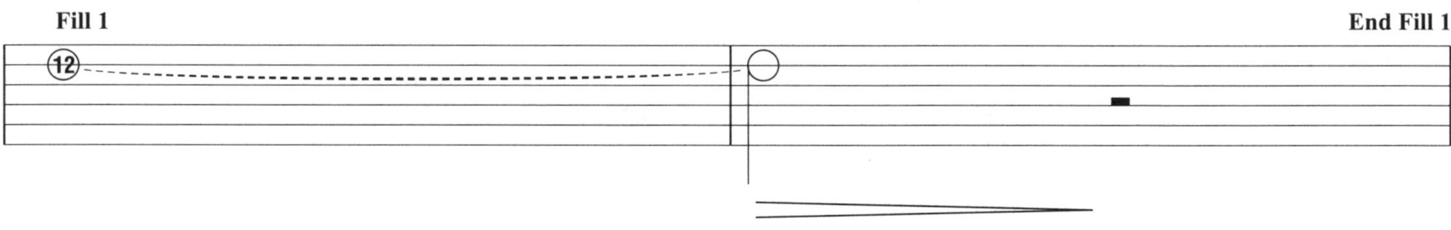

mom locked you in a shed and Un - cle Sam dropped an at - om bomb. But you're

G5 B5 C5 G5 A5 F♯5/C♯

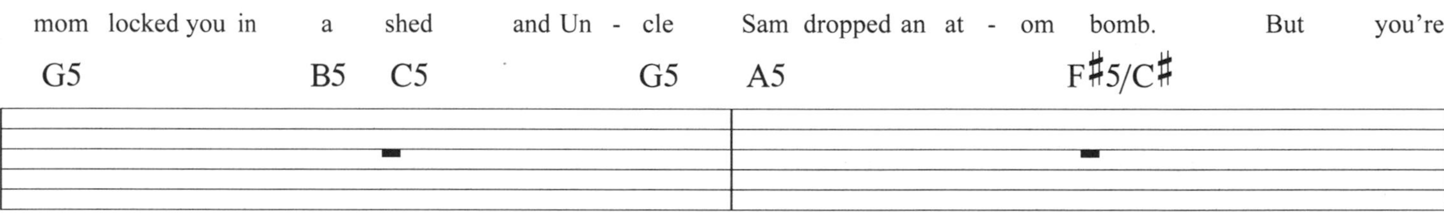

not a-lone; you can let it go and just weep on my breast and

G5 B5 C5 A5 D5

Gtrs. 2 & 3

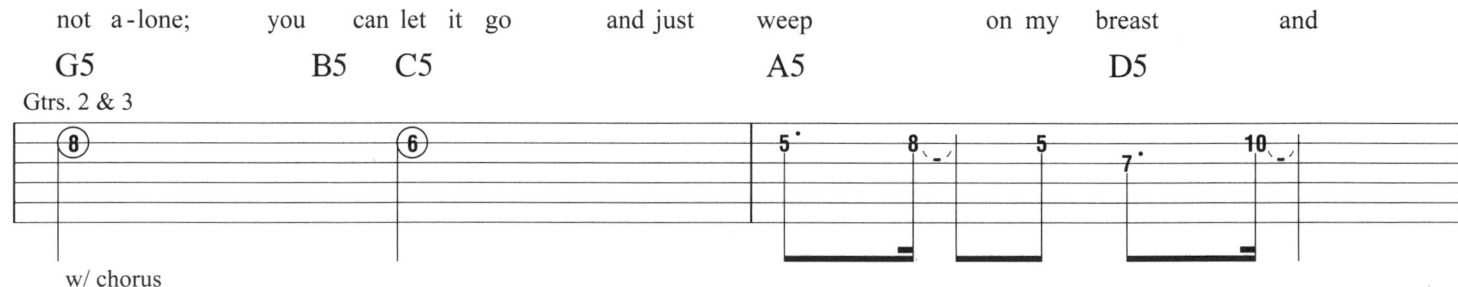

D.S. al Coda 1

cov-er me with your ten-der-ness, and that pain will pass. If I was king

G5 B5 C5 G5 A5 F♯5/C♯

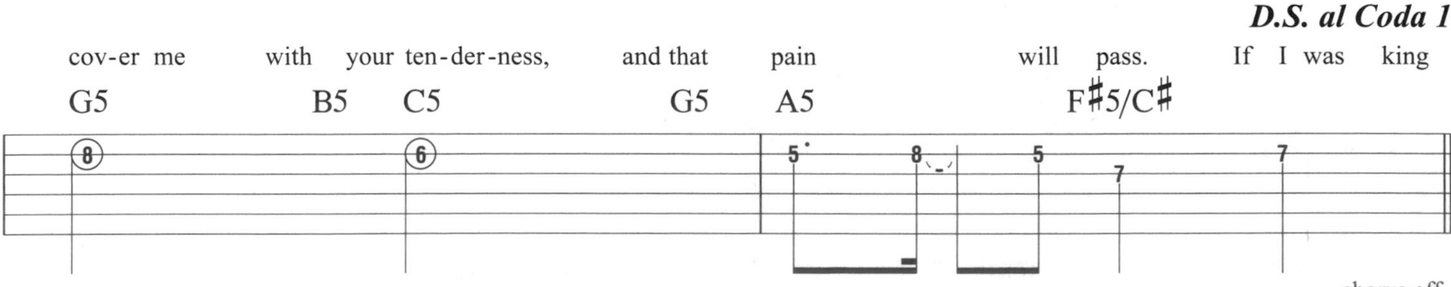

Coda 1

Bridge

Gtr. 3: w/ Fill 1

We are the small fish.

G/B E5 A5 D5 C6

Gtr. 2 **Riff A**

w/ clean tone & reverb

let ring

Gtr. 1 **Rhy. Fig. 3**

slight P.M.

w/ clean tone

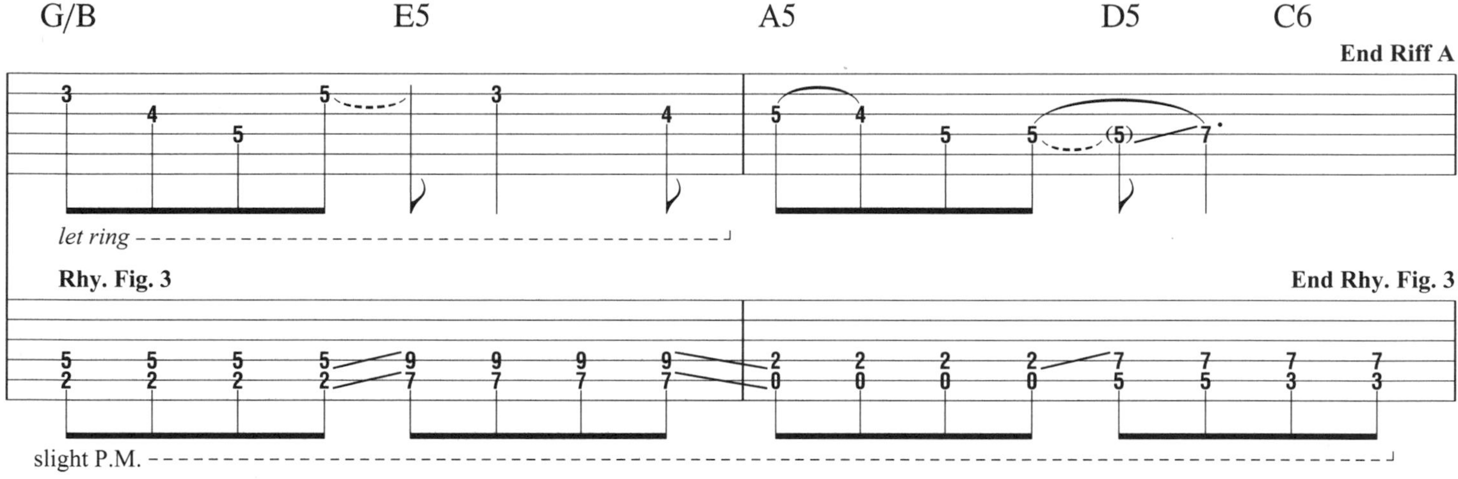

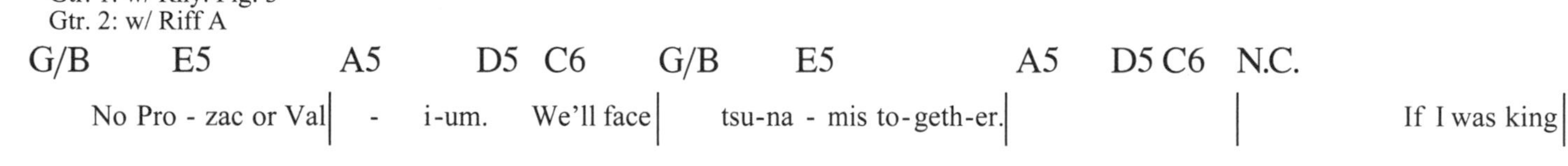

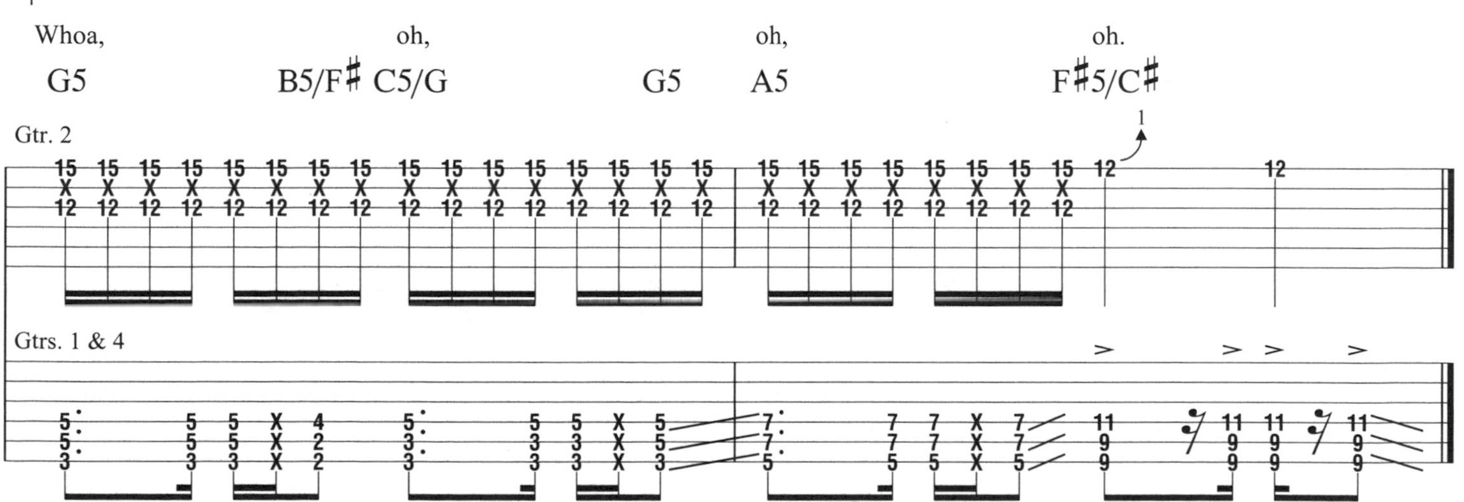

Summer Elaine and Drunk Dori

Words and Music by Rivers Cuomo

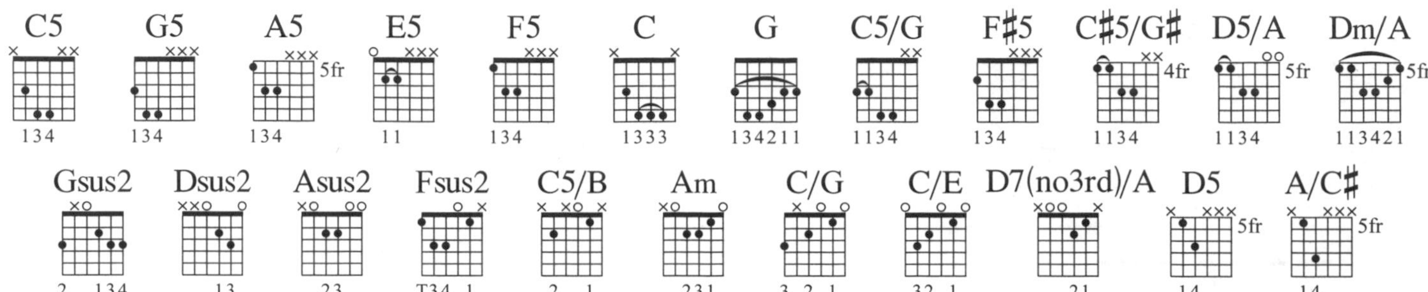

Tune down 1/2 step:
(low to high) E♭-A♭-D♭-G♭-B♭-E♭

Key of C

Intro

Moderately fast ♩ = 128

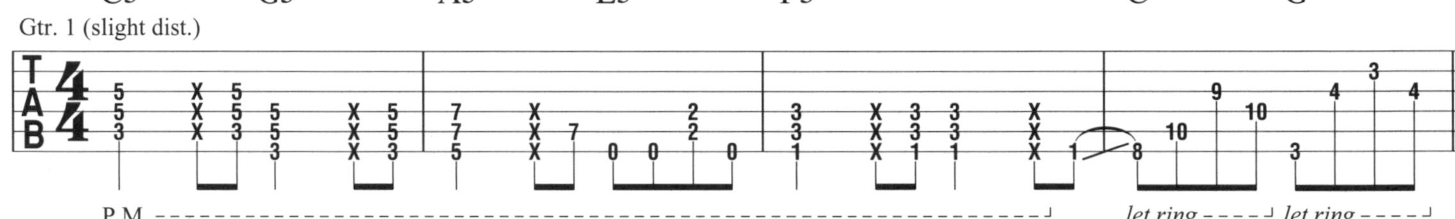

Verse

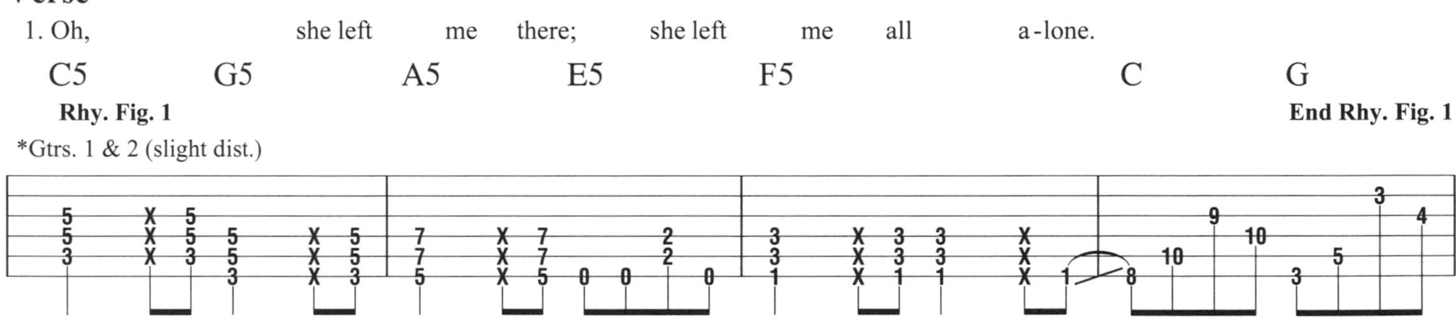

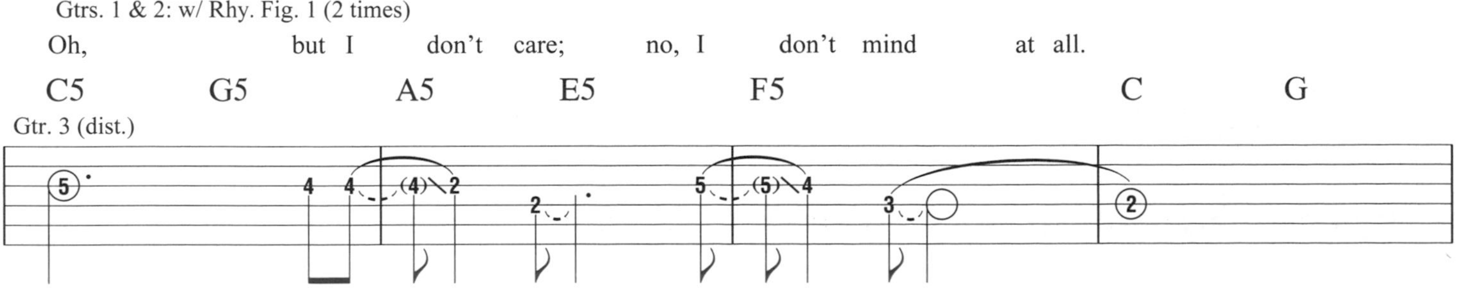

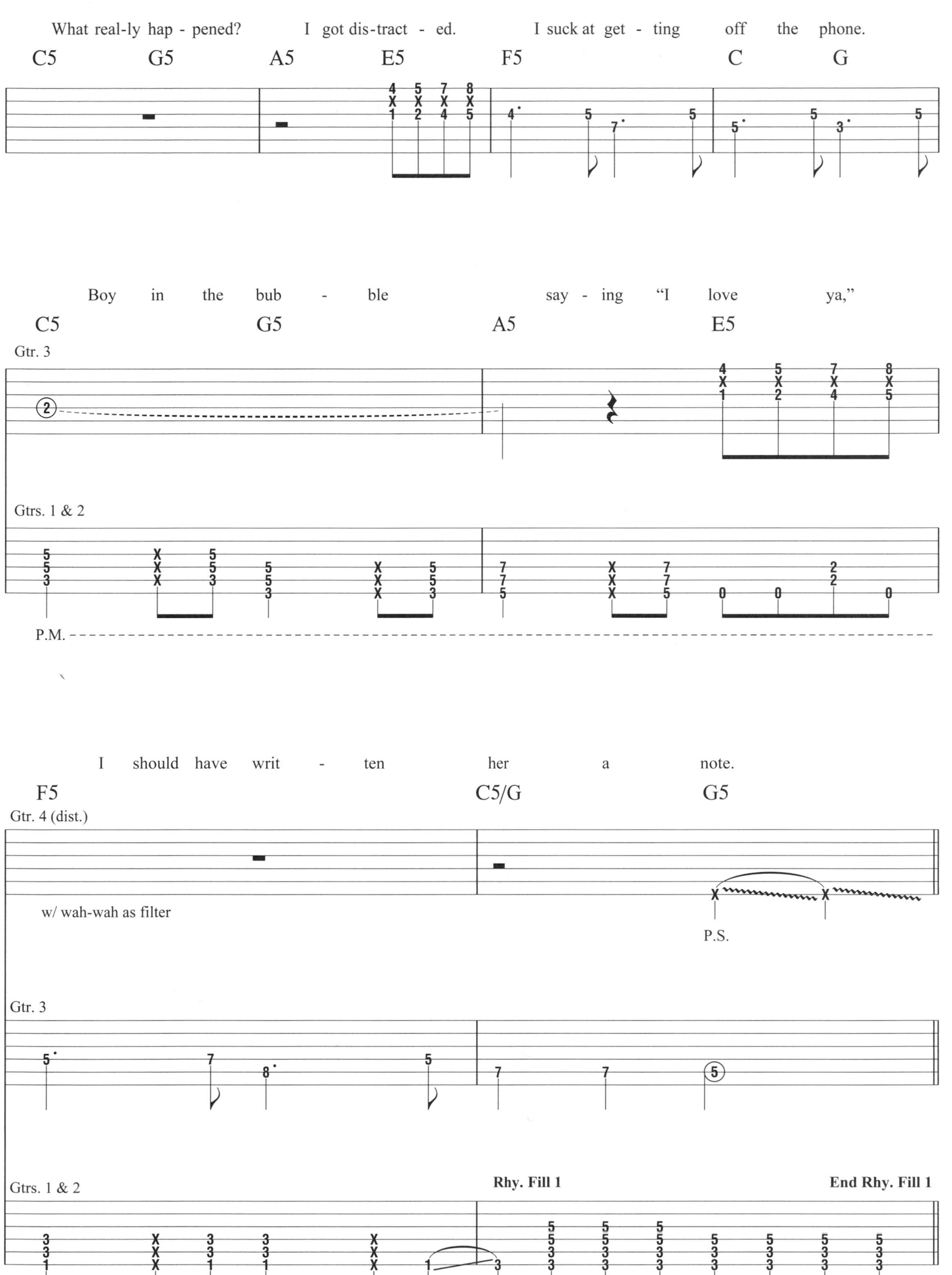
What real-ly hap - pened? I got dis-tract - ed. I suck at get - ting off the phone.
C5 G5 A5 E5 F5 C G
Boy in the bub - ble say - ing "I love ya,"
C5 G5 A5 E5
Gtr. 3
Gtrs. 1 & 2
P.M.
I should have writ - ten her a note.
F5 C5/G G5
Gtr. 4 (dist.)
w/ wah-wah as filter
P.S.
Gtr. 3
Gtrs. 1 & 2
Rhy. Fill 1
End Rhy. Fill 1
P.M.

Key of A

𝄋 Chorus

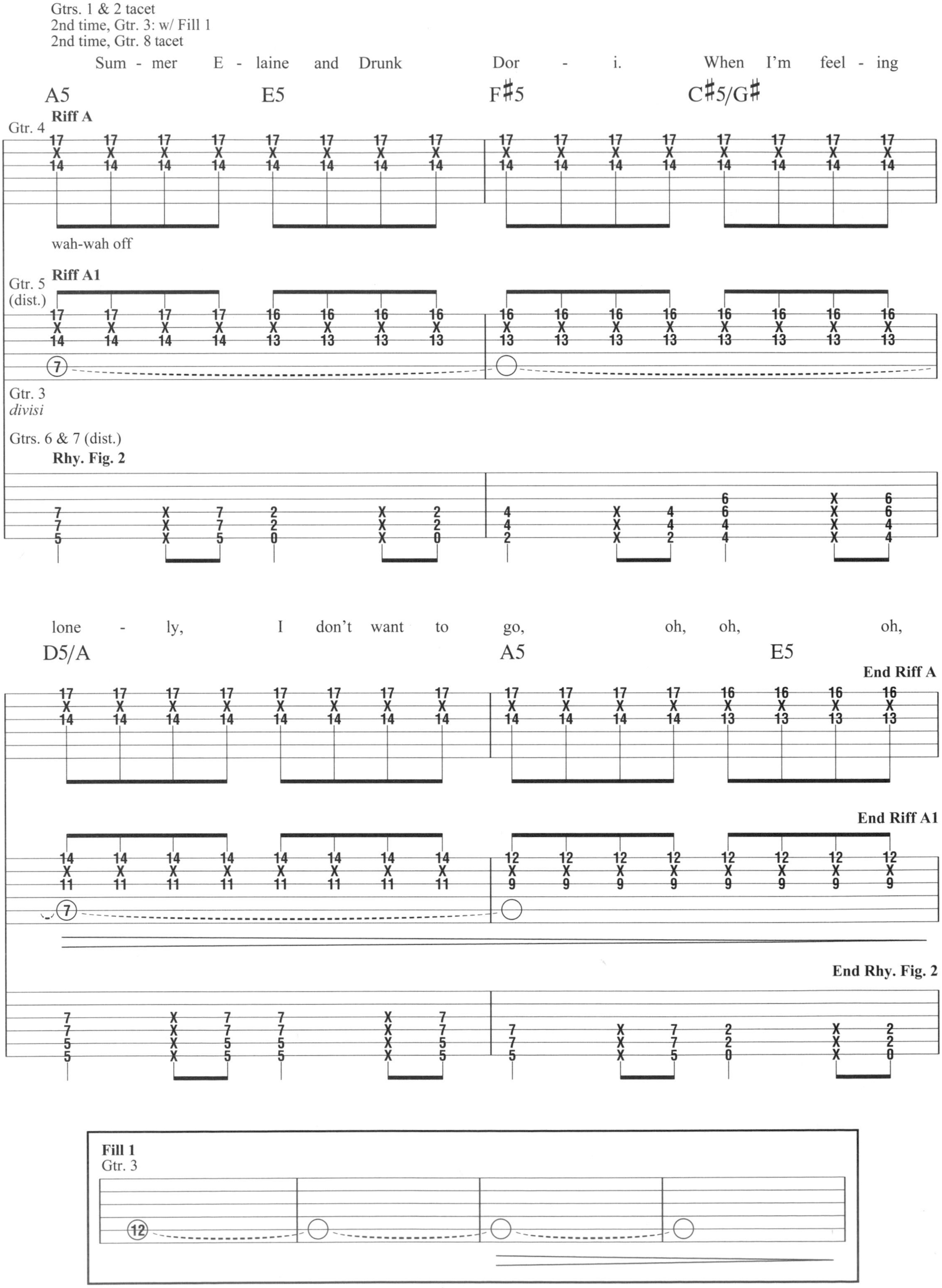

Gtrs. 1 & 2 tacet
2nd time, Gtr. 3: w/ Fill 1
2nd time, Gtr. 8 tacet

Sum - mer E - laine and Drunk Dor - i. When I'm feel - ing

A5 E5 F♯5 C♯5/G♯

Riff A
Gtr. 4

wah-wah off

Riff A1
Gtr. 5 (dist.)

Gtr. 3
divisi

Gtrs. 6 & 7 (dist.)
Rhy. Fig. 2

lone - ly, I don't want to go, oh, oh, oh,

D5/A A5 E5

End Riff A

End Riff A1

End Rhy. Fig. 2

Fill 1
Gtr. 3

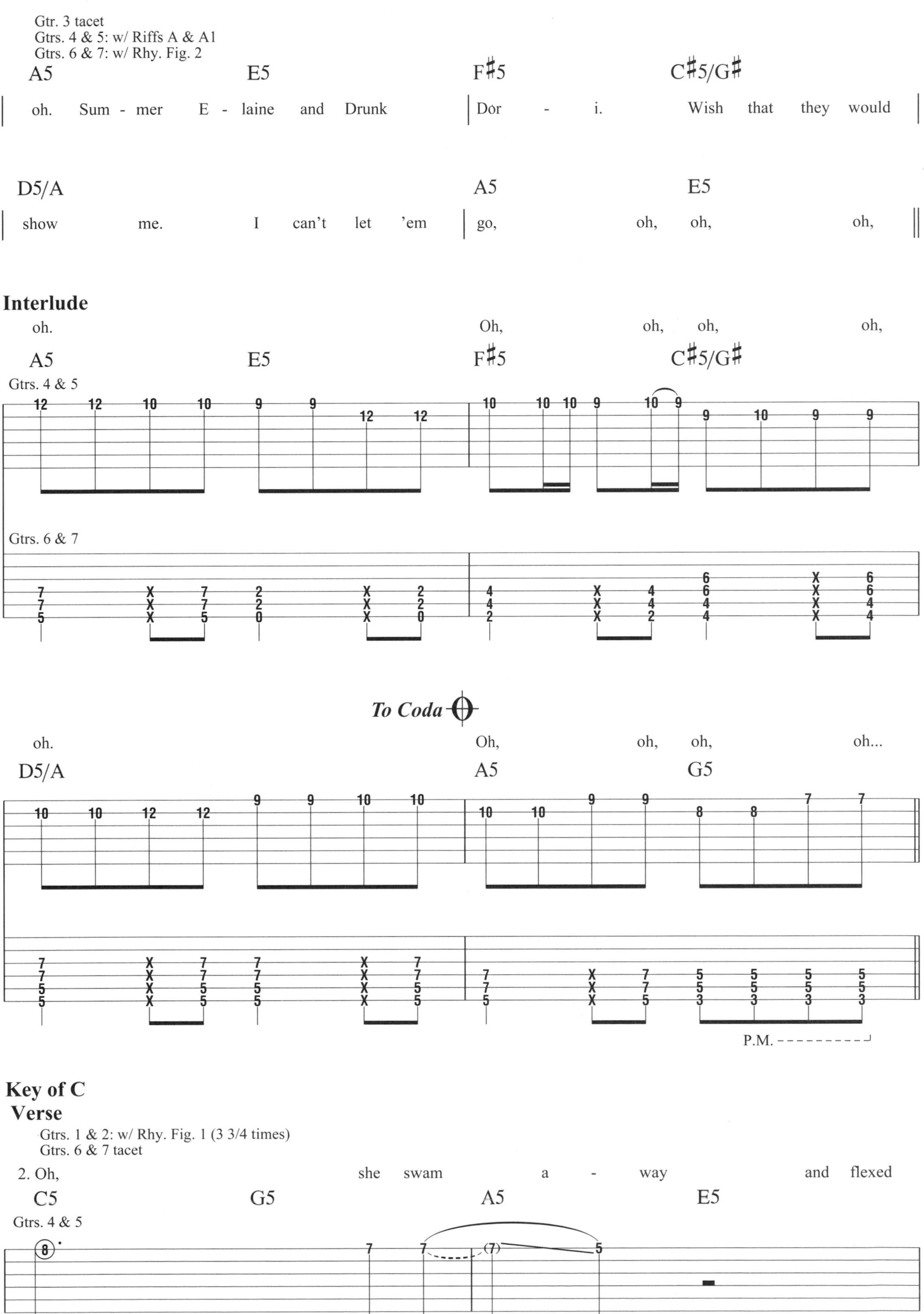

Gtr. 3 tacet
Gtrs. 4 & 5: w/ Riffs A & A1
Gtrs. 6 & 7: w/ Rhy. Fig. 2
A5 E5 F♯5 C♯5/G♯
oh. Sum - mer E - laine and Drunk Dor - i. Wish that they would
D5/A A5 E5
show me. I can't let 'em go, oh, oh, oh,
Interlude
oh. Oh, oh, oh, oh,
A5 E5 F♯5 C♯5/G♯
Gtrs. 4 & 5
Gtrs. 6 & 7
To Coda
oh. Oh, oh, oh, oh...
D5/A A5 G5
P.M.
Key of C
Verse
Gtrs. 1 & 2: w/ Rhy. Fig. 1 (3 3/4 times)
Gtrs. 6 & 7 tacet
2. Oh, she swam a - way and flexed
C5 G5 A5 E5
Gtrs. 4 & 5

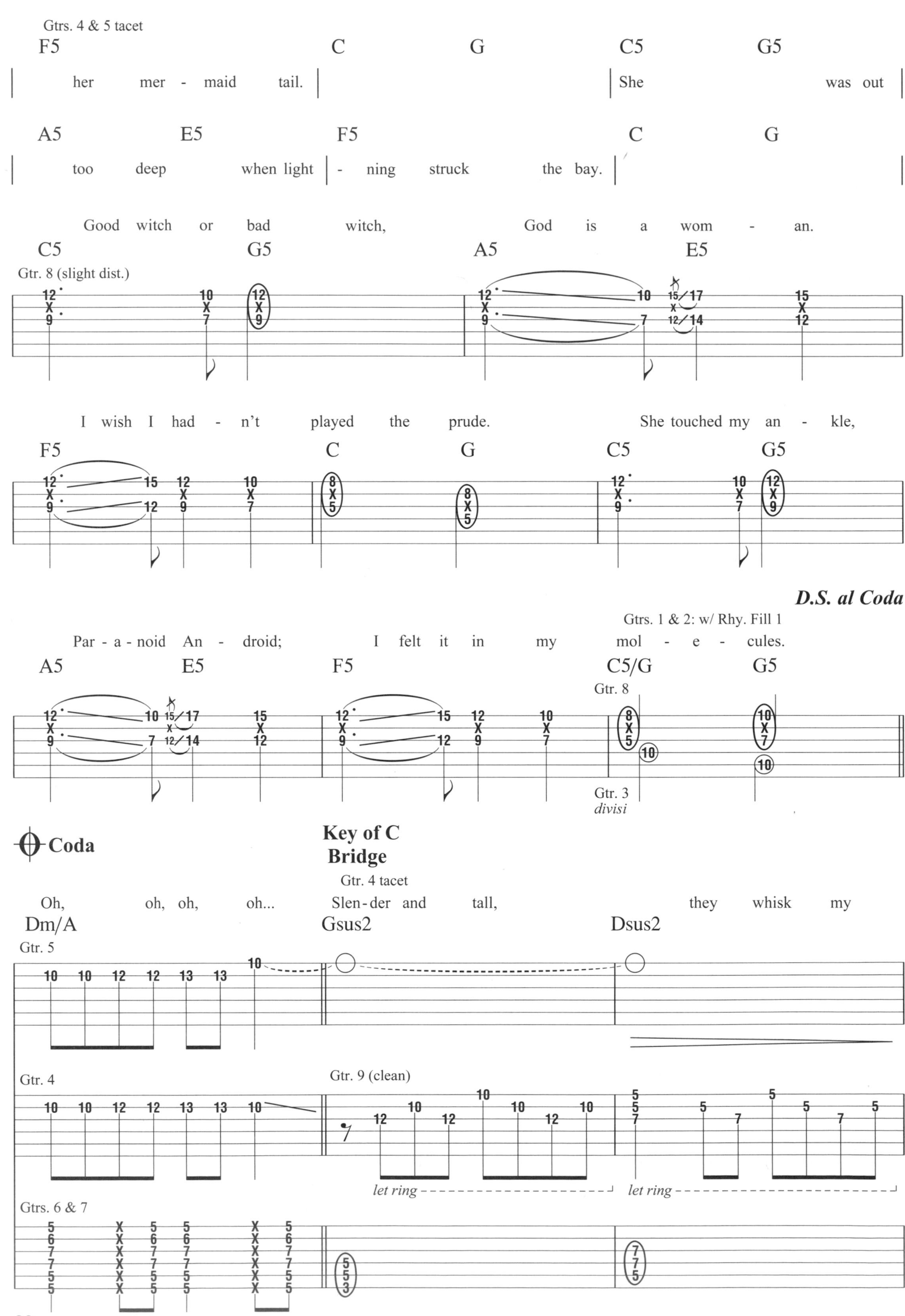

Gtrs. 4 & 5 tacet
F5 C G C5 G5
her mer - maid tail. She was out
A5 E5 F5 C G
too deep when light - ning struck the bay.
Good witch or bad witch, God is a wom - an.
C5 G5 A5 E5
Gtr. 8 (slight dist.)
I wish I had - n't played the prude. She touched my an - kle,
F5 C G C5 G5
D.S. al Coda
Gtrs. 1 & 2: w/ Rhy. Fill 1
Par - a - noid An - droid; I felt it in my mol - e - cules.
A5 E5 F5 C5/G G5
Gtr. 8
Gtr. 3
divisi
Coda
Key of C
Bridge
Gtr. 4 tacet
Oh, oh, oh, oh... Slen - der and tall, they whisk my
Dm/A Gsus2 Dsus2
Gtr. 5
Gtr. 4
Gtr. 9 (clean)
let ring
let ring
Gtrs. 6 & 7

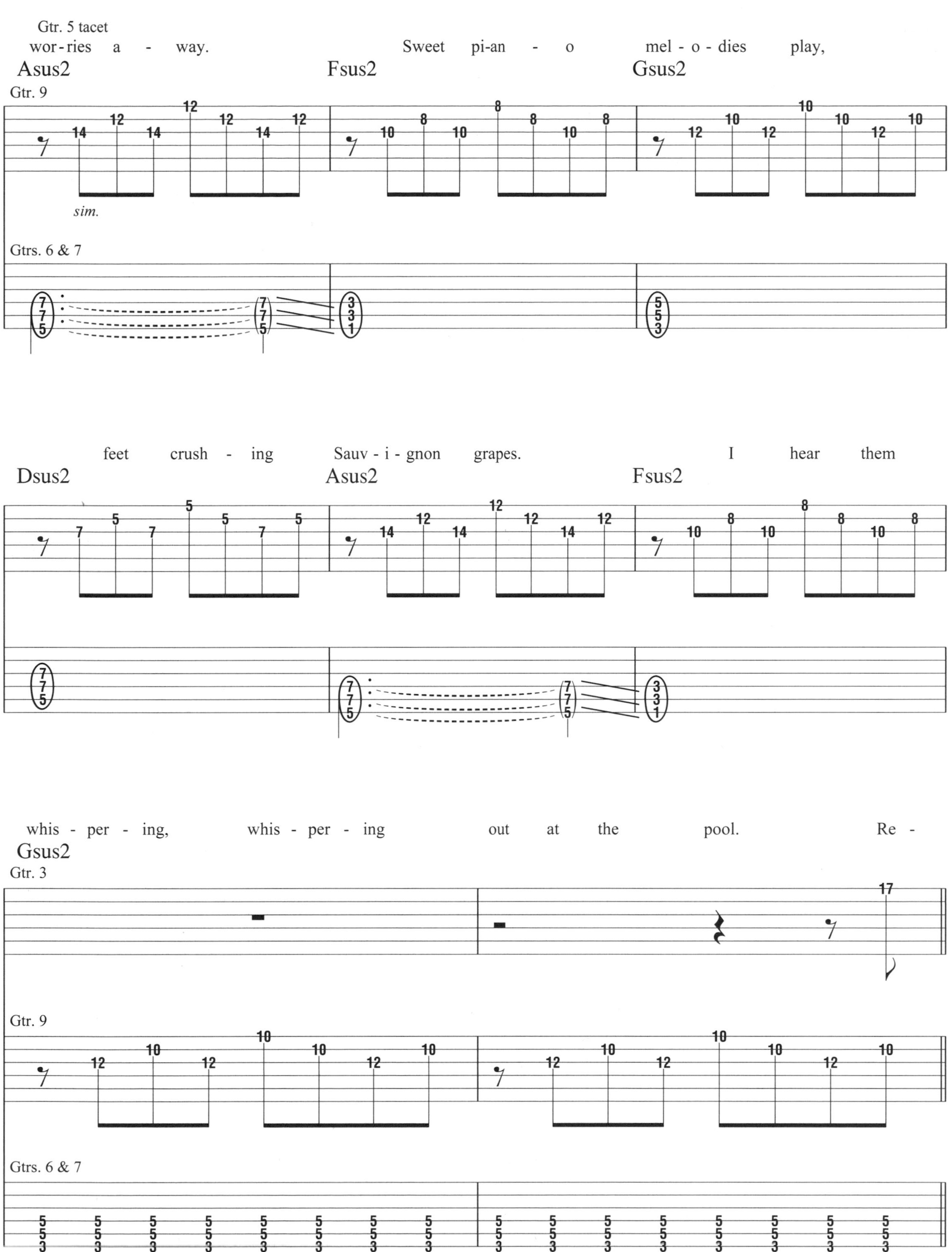
Gtr. 5 tacet
wor - ries a - way. Sweet pi-an - o mel - o - dies play,
Asus2
Fsus2
Gsus2
Gtr. 9
sim.
Gtrs. 6 & 7
feet crush - ing Sauv - i - gnon grapes. I hear them
Dsus2
Asus2
Fsus2
whis - per - ing, whis - per - ing out at the pool. Re -
Gsus2
Gtr. 3
Gtr. 9
Gtrs. 6 & 7

Bridge

Half-time feel

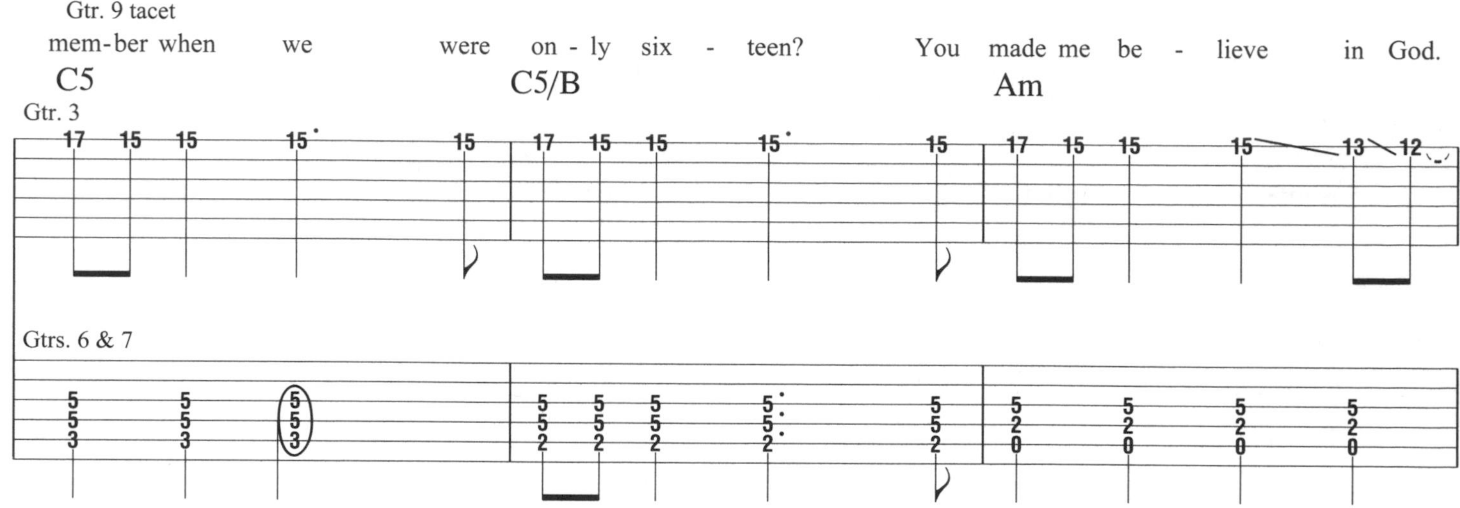

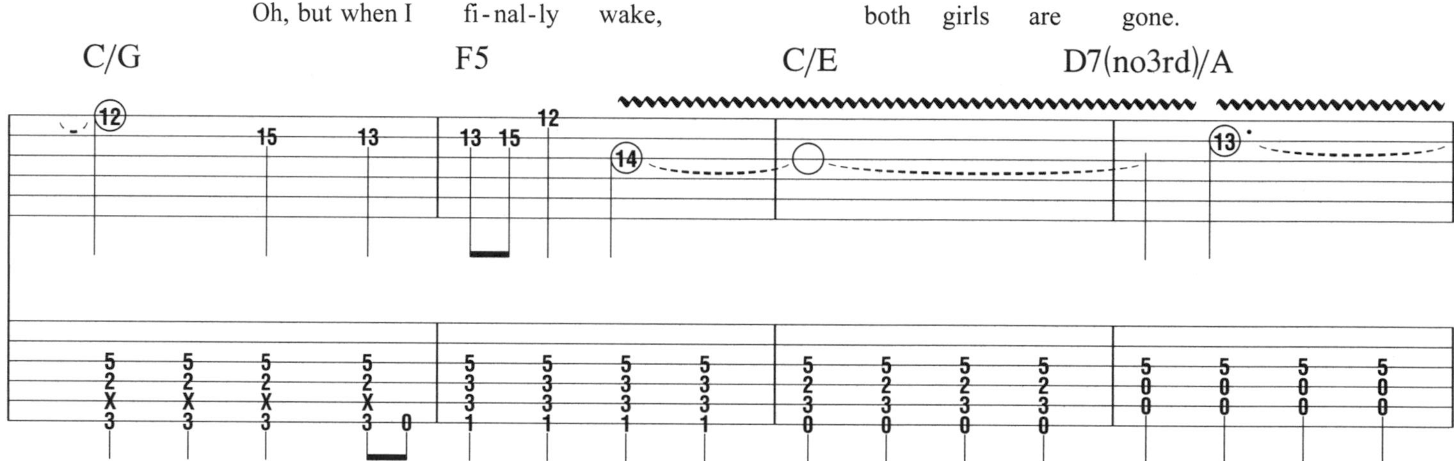

Key of A

Guitar Solo

End half-time feel

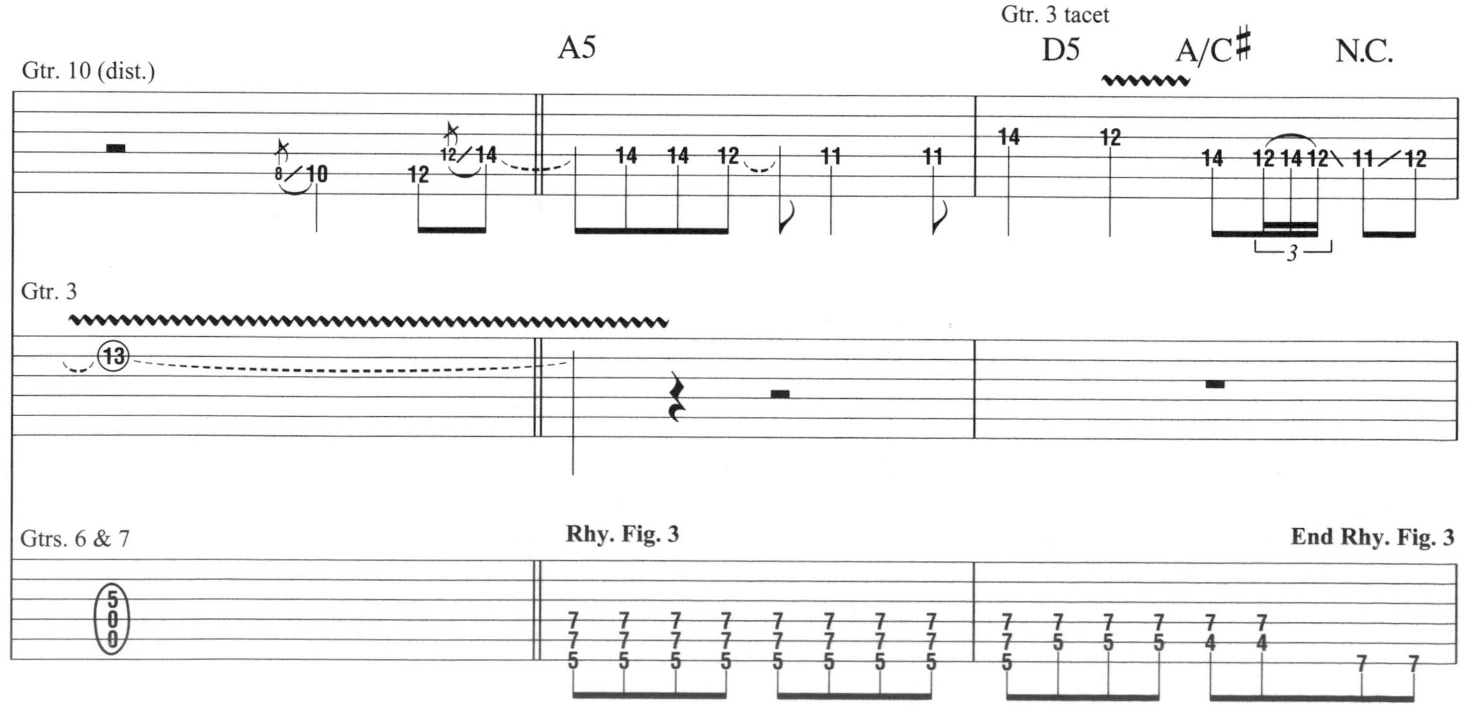

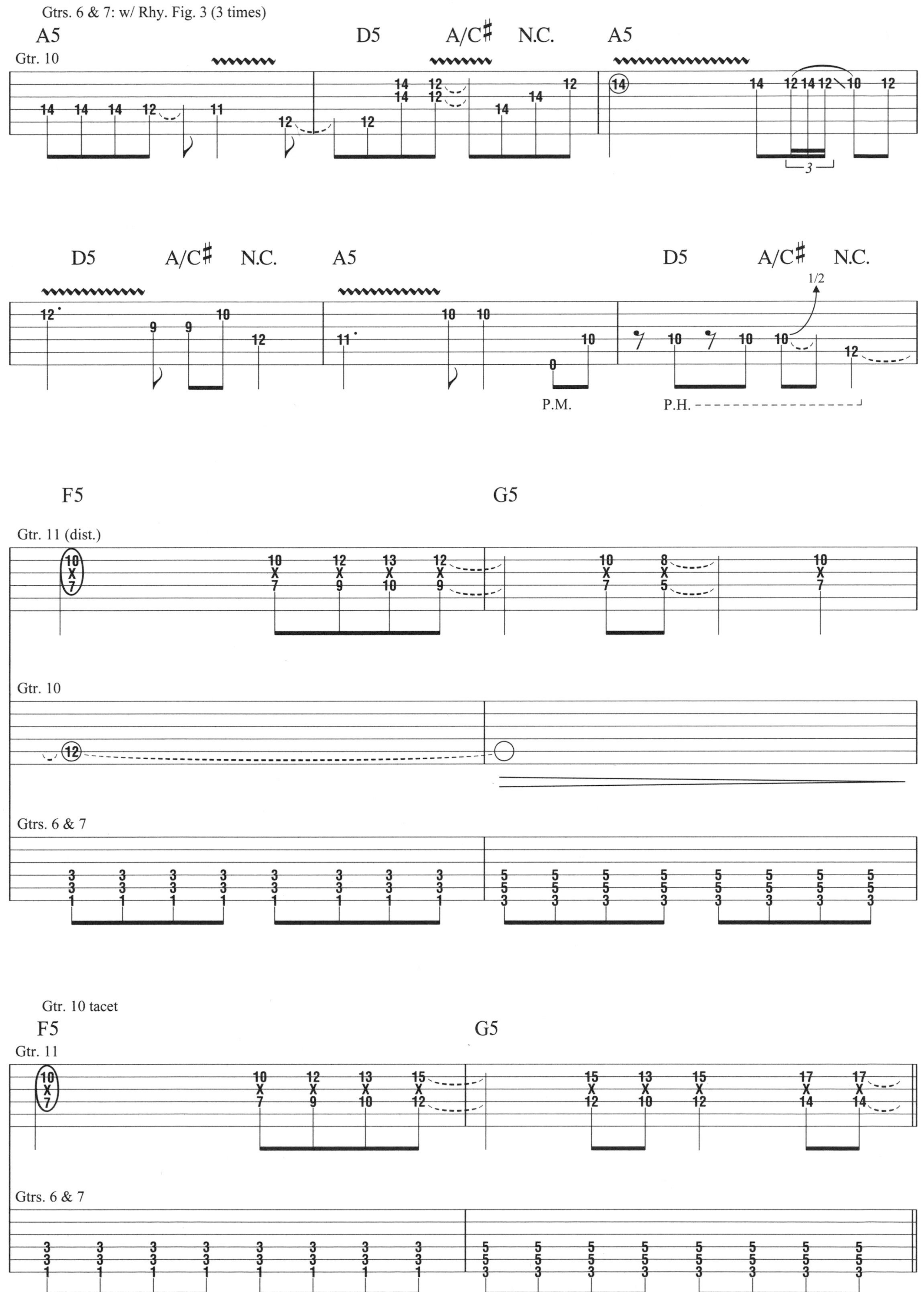

Gtrs. 6 & 7: w/ Rhy. Fig. 3 (3 times)
A5
D5
A/C♯
N.C.
A5
Gtr. 10
D5
A/C♯
N.C.
A5
D5
A/C♯
N.C.
1/2
P.M.
P.H.
F5
G5
Gtr. 11 (dist.)
Gtr. 10
Gtrs. 6 & 7
Gtr. 10 tacet
F5
G5
Gtr. 11
Gtrs. 6 & 7

Chorus
Gtrs. 4 & 5: w/ Riff A (2 times)
Gtrs. 6 & 7: w/ Rhy. Fig. 2 (2 3/4 times)
Sum - mer E - laine and Drunk Dor - i. When I'm feel - ing
A5 E5 F♯5 C♯5/G♯
Gtr. 11
lone - ly, I don't want to go, oh, oh, oh,
D5/A A5 E5
Gtr. 11 tacet
A5 E5 F♯5 C♯5/G♯
oh, Sum - mer E - laine and Drunk Dor - i. Wish that they would
D5/A A5 E5
show me. I can't let 'em go, oh, oh, oh,
Outro
oh. (Oh, oh. Oh, oh.) Oh, oh, oh, oh, oh. (Oh, oh. Oh, oh.)
A5 E5 F♯5 C♯5/G♯ D5/A
Gtrs. 4 & 5
Oh, oh, oh, oh, oh.
A5 E5 A5 N.C.
Gtrs. 4 & 5
w/ tremolo
Gtrs. 6 & 7

L.A. Girlz

Words and Music by Rivers Cuomo, Brian Bell and Luther Russell

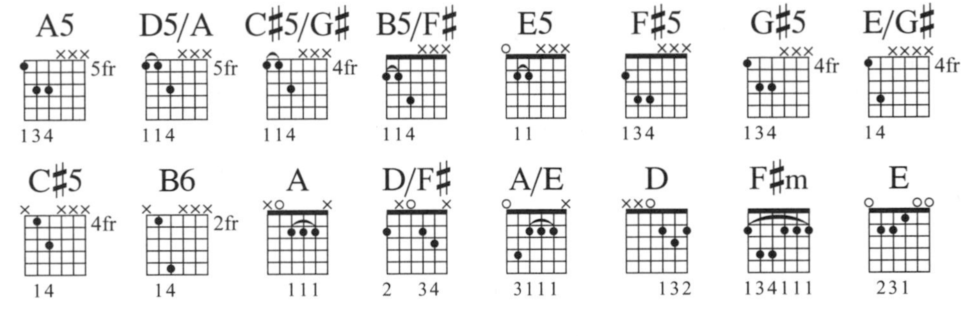

Tune down 1/2 step:
(low to high) E♭-A♭-D♭-G♭-B♭-E♭

Key of A

Chorus

Moderately slow ♩. = 84

L. - A. girls, please act your age. You

A5 D5/A C♯5/G♯

Rhy. Fig. 1

*Gtr. 1 (dist.)

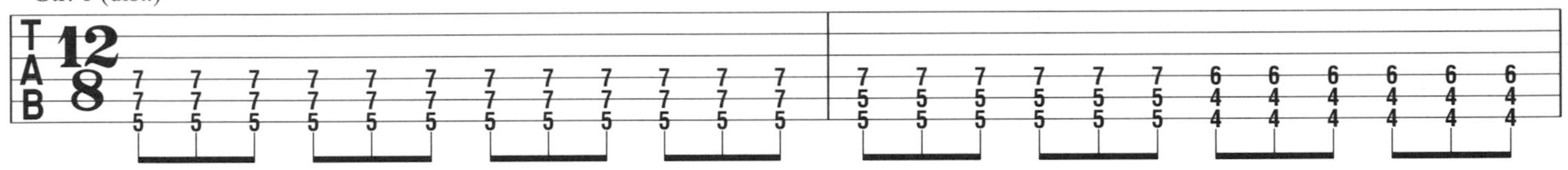

*Doubled throughout

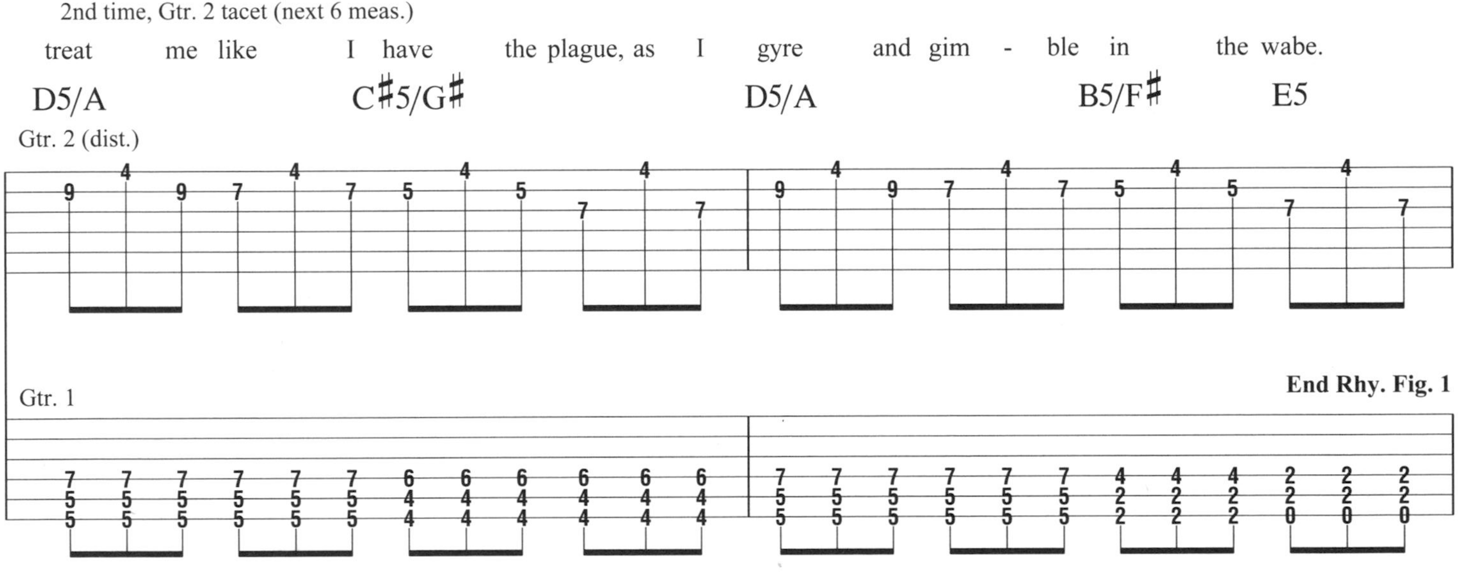

Gtr. 1: w/ Rhy. Fig. 1

L. - A. girls, please act your age.

A5 D5/A C♯5/G♯

Gtr. 2

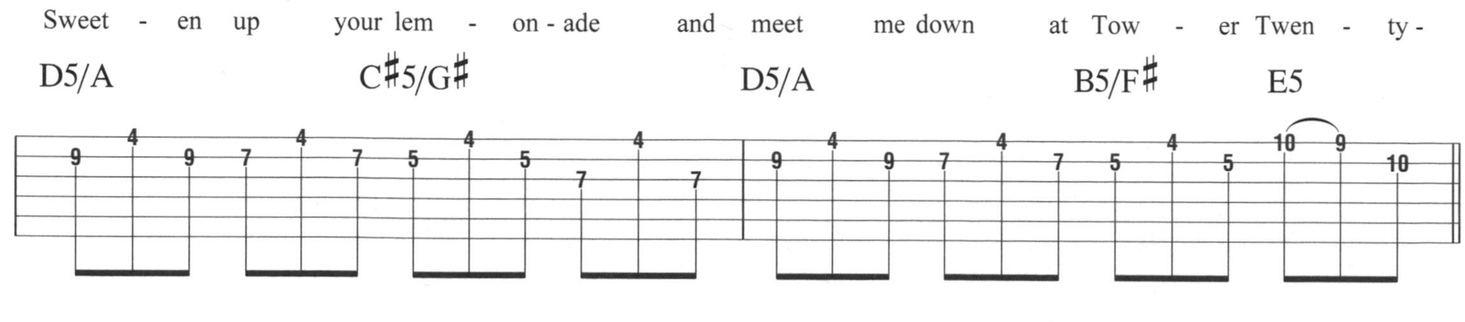
Sweet - en up your lem - on - ade and meet me down at Tow - er Twen - ty -
D5/A
C♯5/G♯
D5/A
B5/F♯
E5

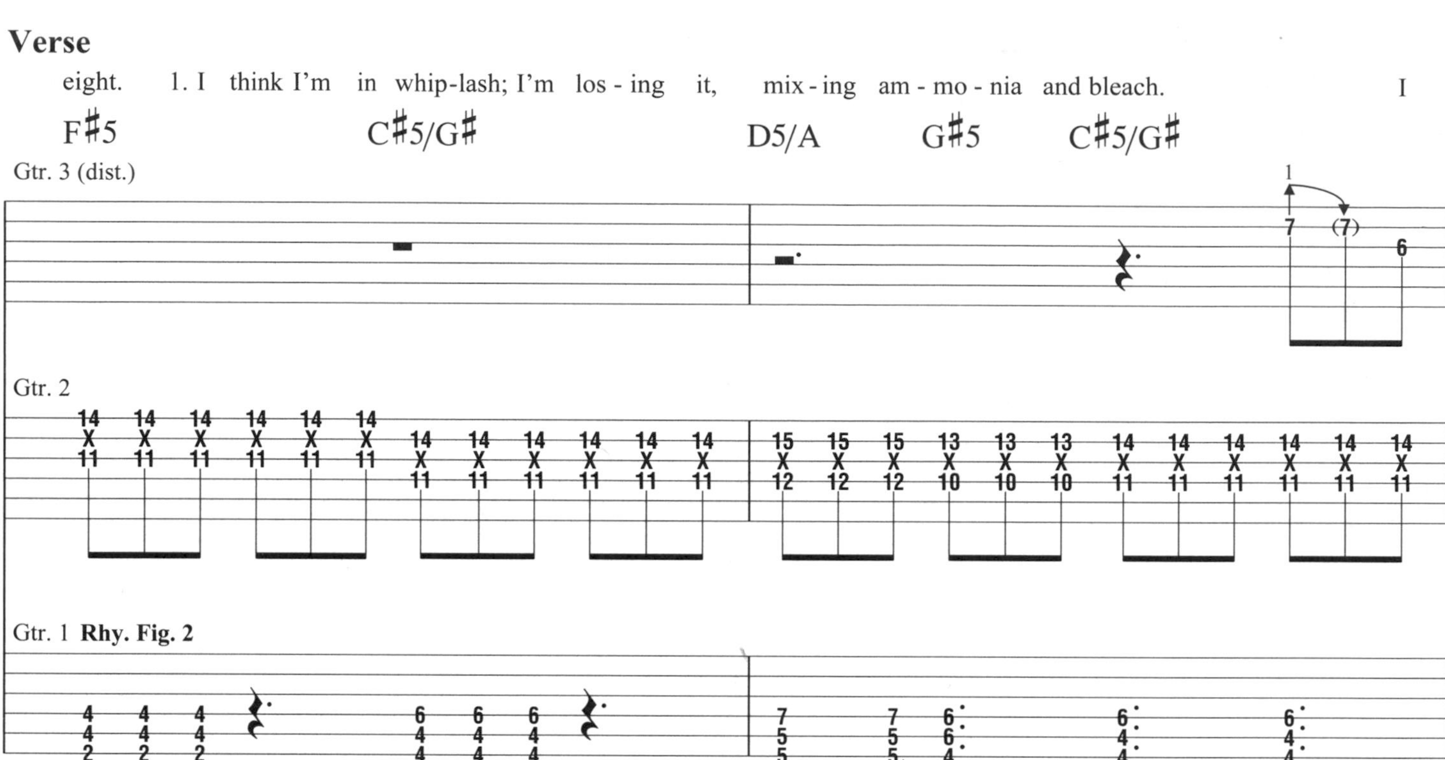
Verse
eight. 1. I think I'm in whip-lash; I'm los - ing it, mix - ing am - mo - nia and bleach. I
F♯5
C♯5/G♯
D5/A
G♯5
C♯5/G♯
Gtr. 3 (dist.)
Gtr. 2
Gtr. 1 Rhy. Fig. 2

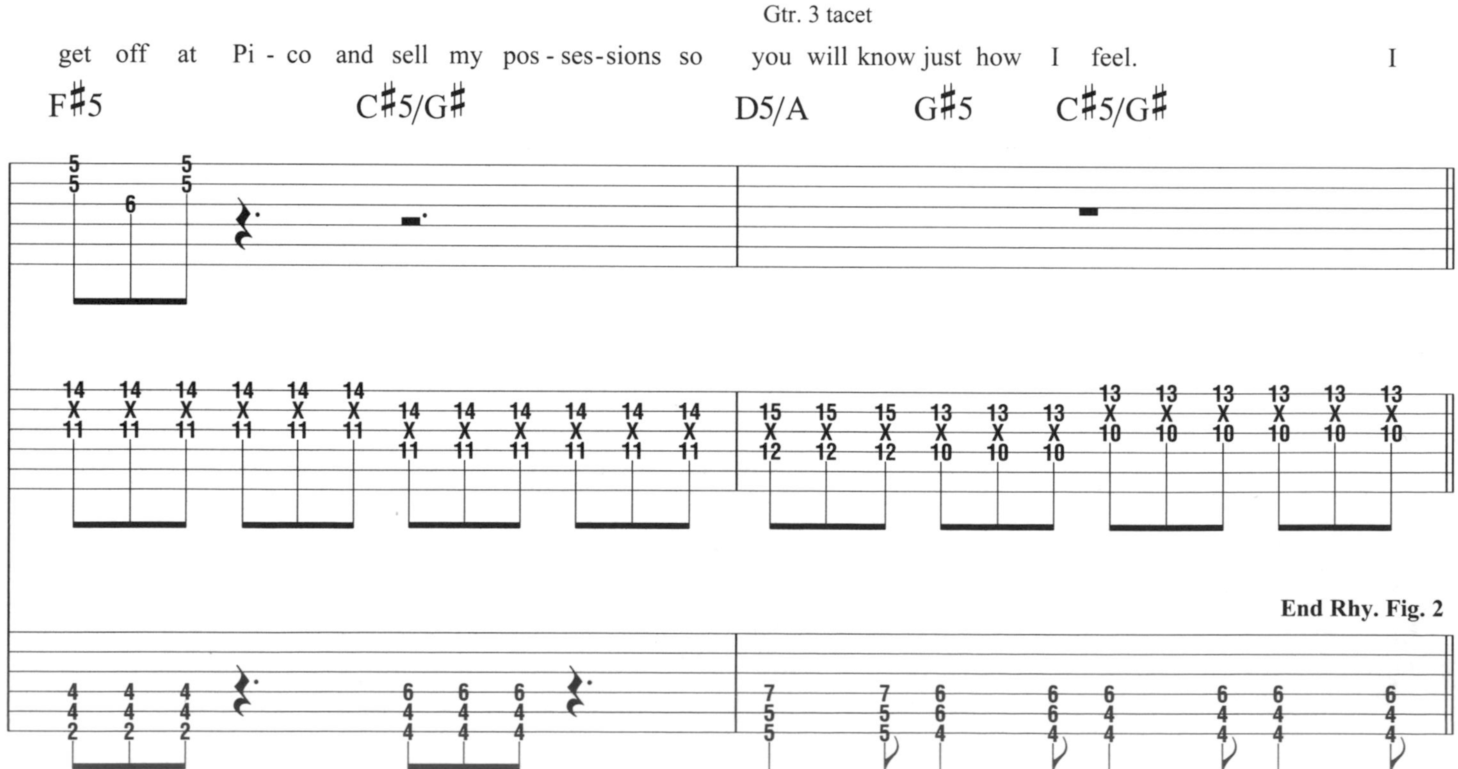
Gtr. 3 tacet
get off at Pi - co and sell my pos - ses - sions so you will know just how I feel. I
F♯5
C♯5/G♯
D5/A
G♯5
C♯5/G♯
End Rhy. Fig. 2

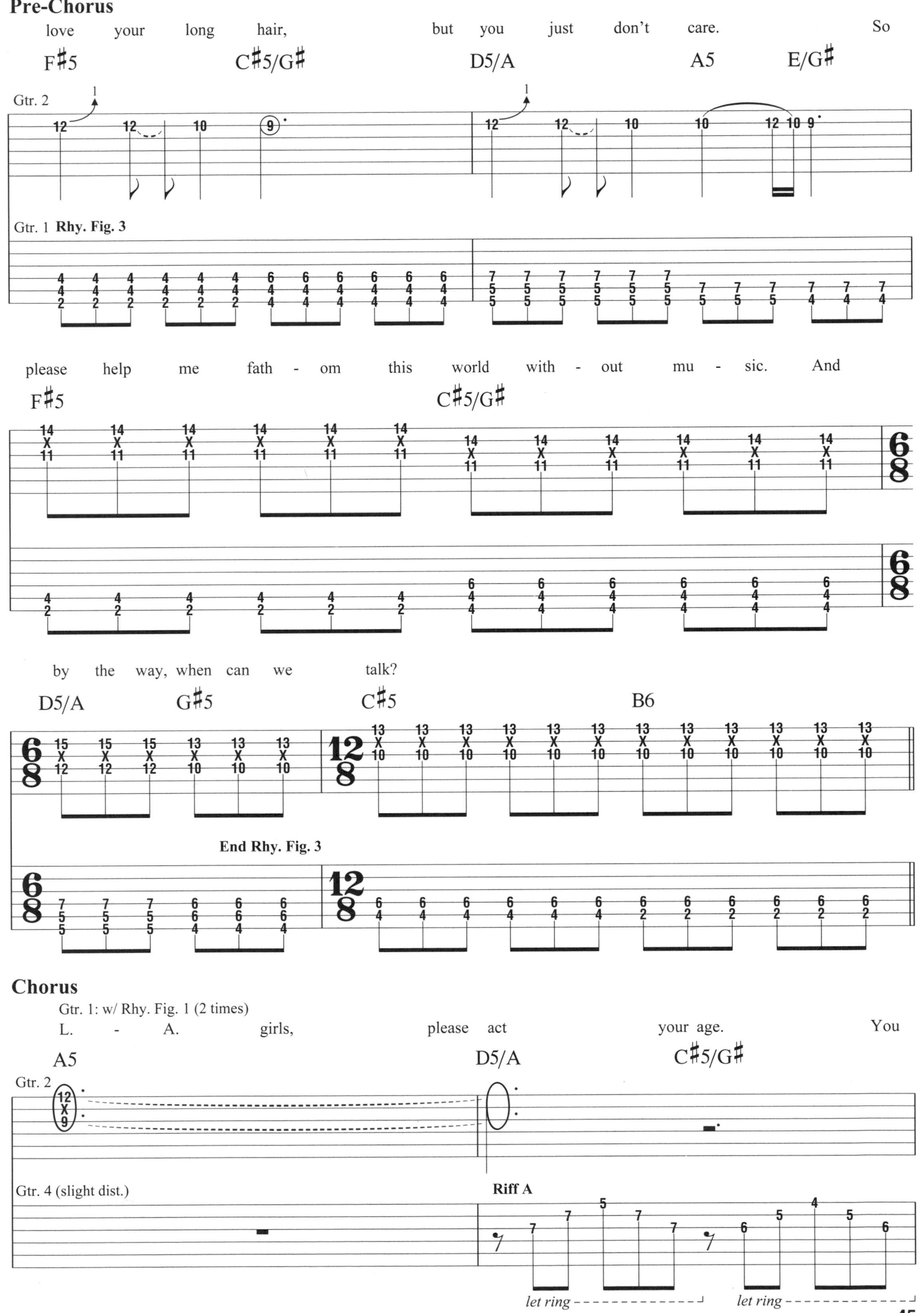
Pre-Chorus
love your long hair, but you just don't care. So
F♯5 C♯5/G♯ D5/A A5 E/G♯
Gtr. 2
Gtr. 1 Rhy. Fig. 3
please help me fath - om this world with - out mu - sic. And
F♯5 C♯5/G♯
by the way, when can we talk?
D5/A G♯5 C♯5 B6
End Rhy. Fig. 3
Chorus
Gtr. 1: w/ Rhy. Fig. 1 (2 times)
L. - A. girls, please act your age. You
A5 D5/A C♯5/G♯
Gtr. 2
Gtr. 4 (slight dist.)
Riff A
let ring
let ring

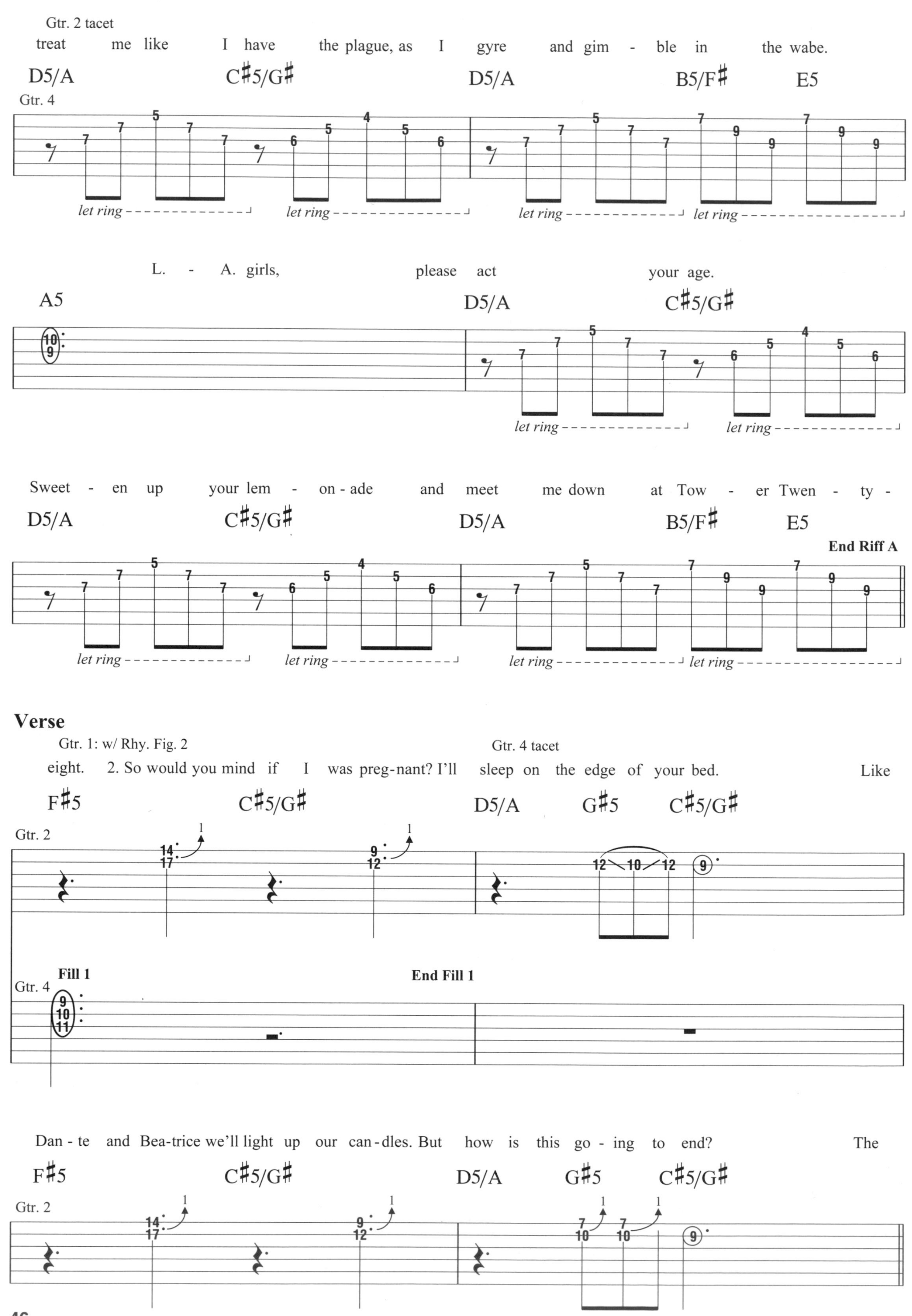

Gtr. 2 tacet
treat me like I have the plague, as I gyre and gim - ble in the wabe.
D5/A C♯5/G♯ D5/A B5/F♯ E5
Gtr. 4
let ring
L. - A. girls, please act your age.
A5 D5/A C♯5/G♯
Sweet - en up your lem - on - ade and meet me down at Tow - er Twen - ty -
D5/A C♯5/G♯ D5/A B5/F♯ E5
End Riff A
Verse
Gtr. 1: w/ Rhy. Fig. 2
Gtr. 4 tacet
eight. 2. So would you mind if I was preg-nant? I'll sleep on the edge of your bed. Like
F♯5 C♯5/G♯ D5/A G♯5 C♯5/G♯
Gtr. 2
Fill 1
End Fill 1
Gtr. 4
Dan - te and Bea-trice we'll light up our can-dles. But how is this go - ing to end? The
F♯5 C♯5/G♯ D5/A G♯5 C♯5/G♯
Gtr. 2

Pre-Chorus

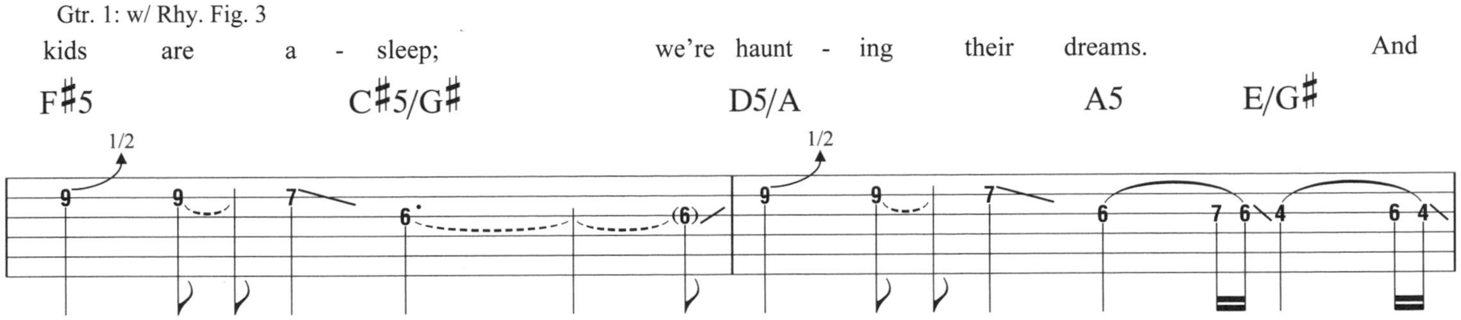

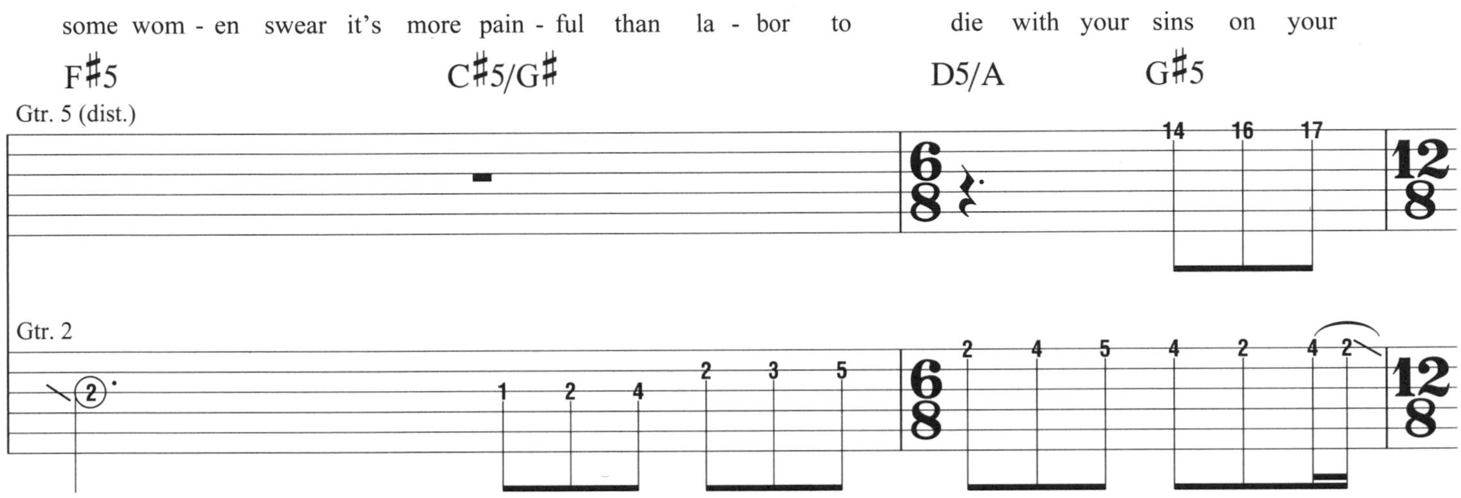

Gtr. 1: w/ Rhy. Fig. 3

kids are a - sleep; we're haunt - ing their dreams. And

F♯5 C♯5/G♯ D5/A A5 E/G♯

some wom - en swear it's more pain - ful than la - bor to die with your sins on your

F♯5 C♯5/G♯ D5/A G♯5

Gtr. 5 (dist.)

Gtr. 2

Bridge

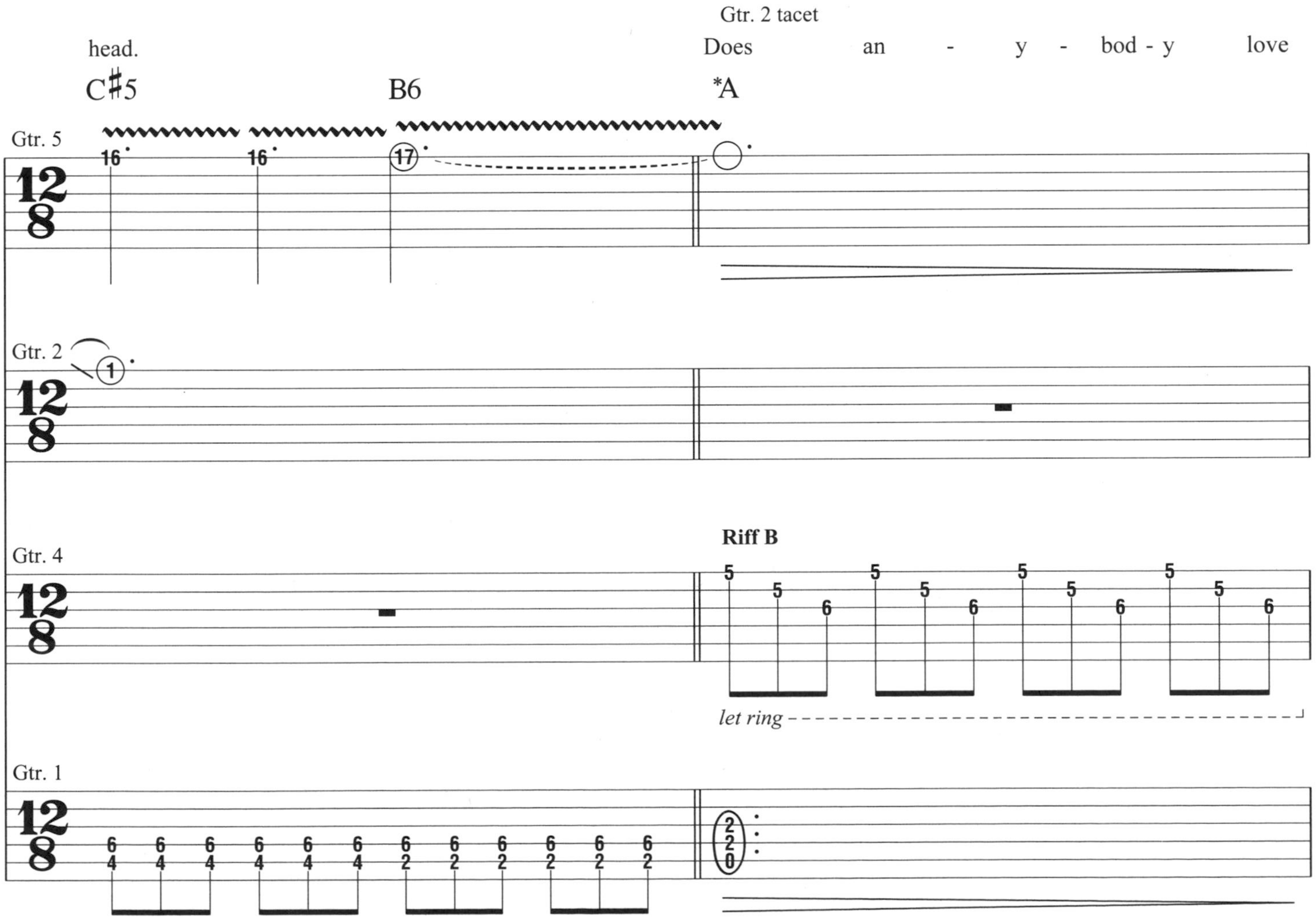

Gtr. 2 tacet

head. Does an - y - bod - y love

C♯5 B6 *A

Gtr. 5

Gtr. 2

Gtr. 4

Riff B

let ring

Gtr. 1

*Chord symbols reflect overall harmony.

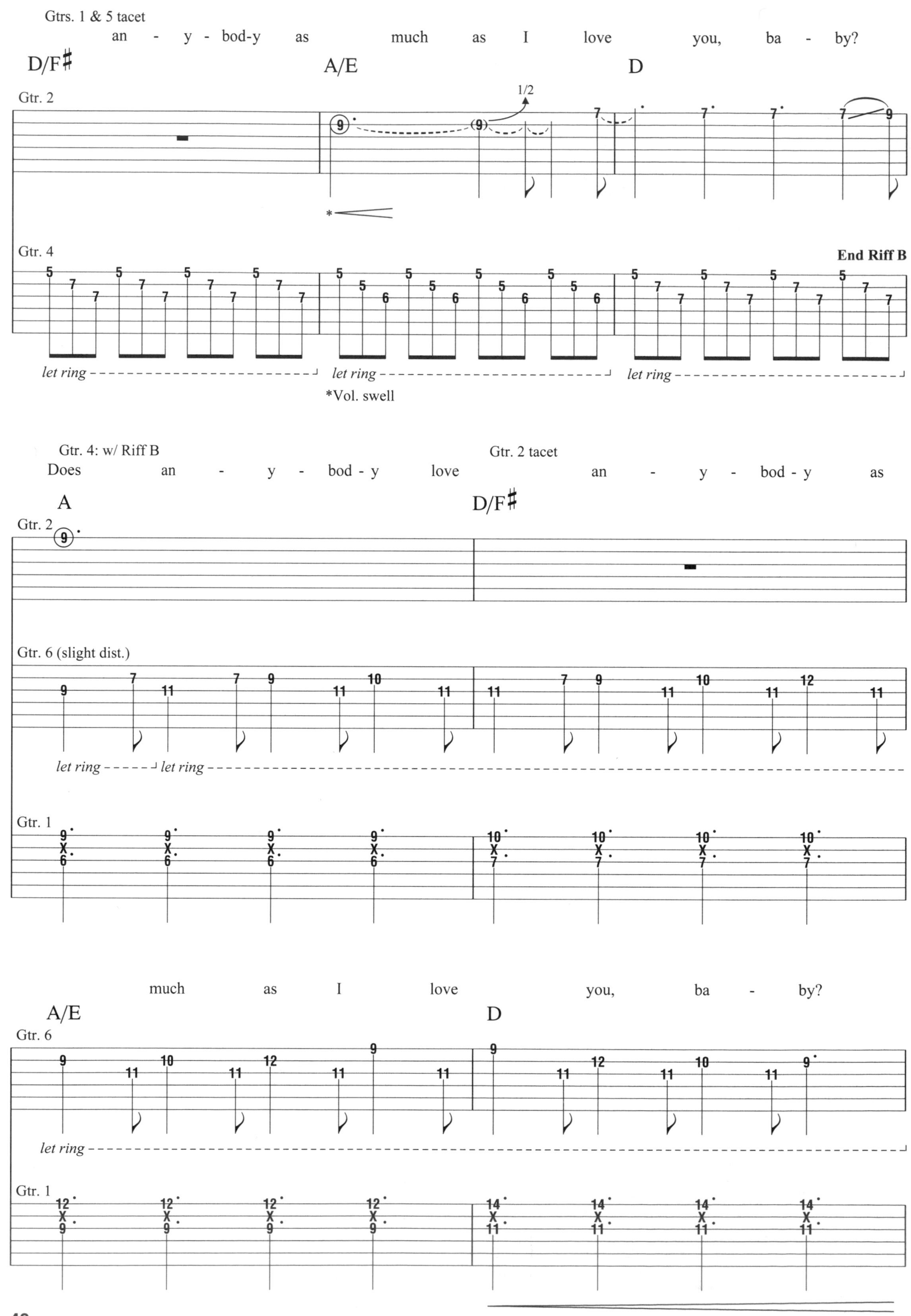

Gtrs. 1 & 5 tacet
an - y - bod-y as much as I love you, ba - by?
D/F♯
A/E
D
Gtr. 2
1/2
Gtr. 4
End Riff B
let ring
*Vol. swell
Gtr. 4: w/ Riff B
Gtr. 2 tacet
Does an - y - bod - y love an - y - bod - y as
A
D/F♯
Gtr. 6 (slight dist.)
Gtr. 1
much as I love you, ba - by?
A/E
D

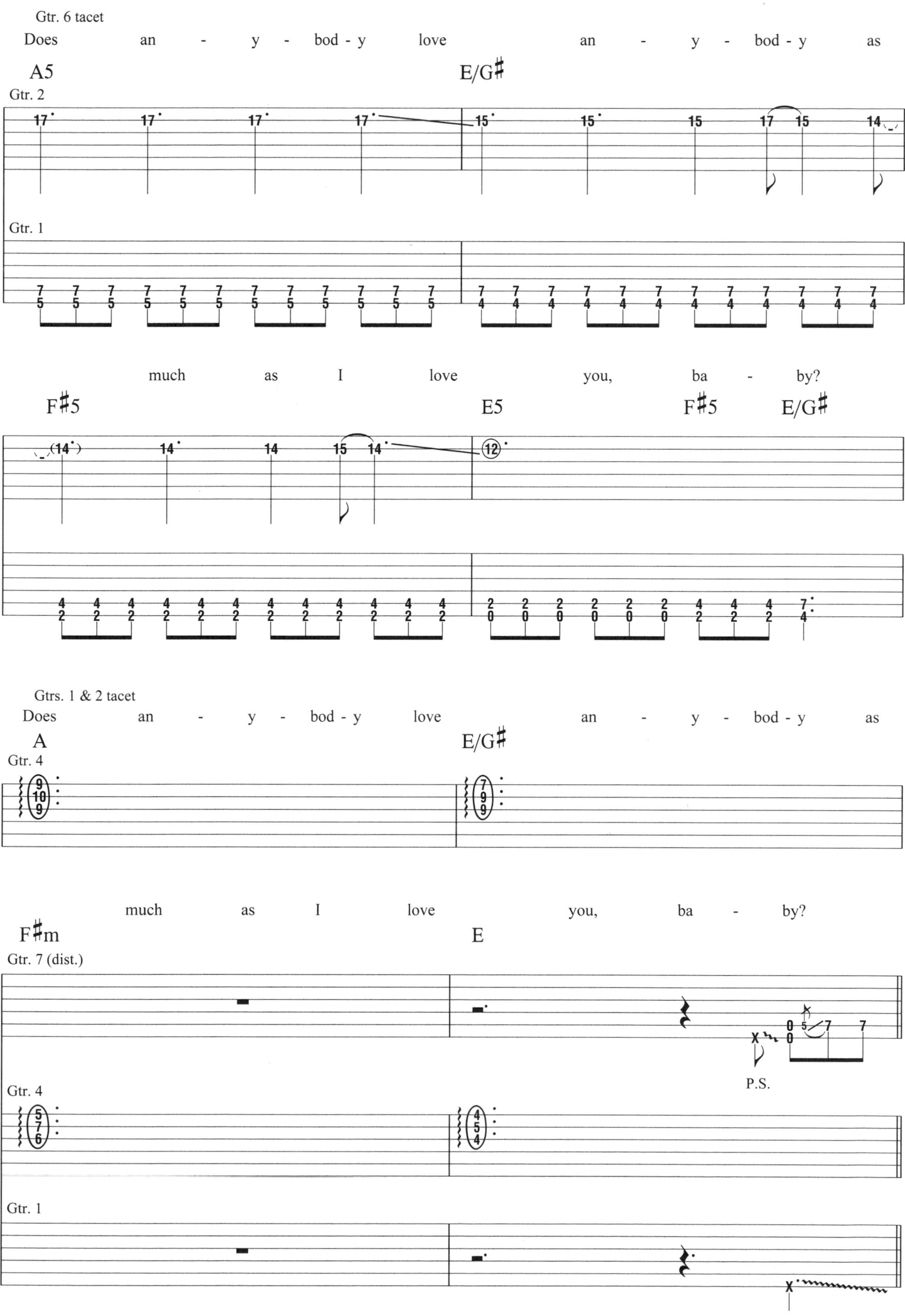
Gtr. 6 tacet
Does an - y - bod - y love an - y - bod - y as
A5
E/G♯
Gtr. 2
Gtr. 1
much as I love you, ba - by?
F♯5
E5
F♯5
E/G♯
Gtrs. 1 & 2 tacet
Does an - y - bod - y love an - y - bod - y as
A
E/G♯
Gtr. 4
much as I love you, ba - by?
F♯m
E
Gtr. 7 (dist.)
P.S.
Gtr. 4
Gtr. 1
P.S.

Guitar Solo

Gtr. 1: w/ Rhy. Fig. 1 (2 times)
Gtr. 4 tacet

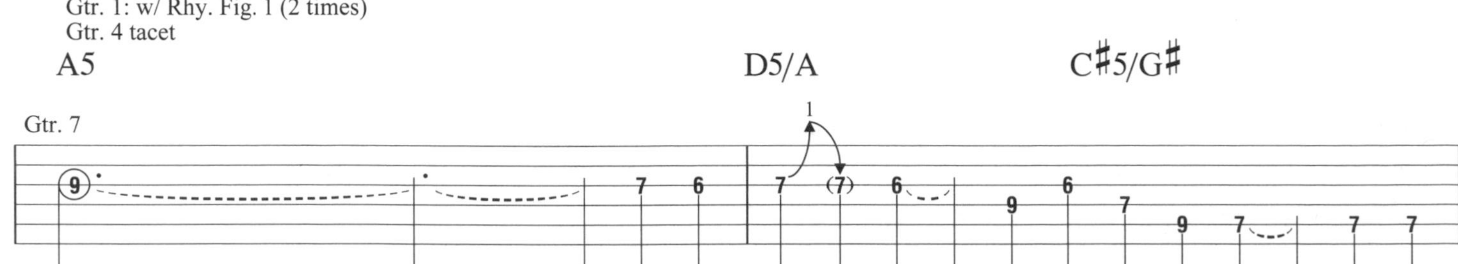

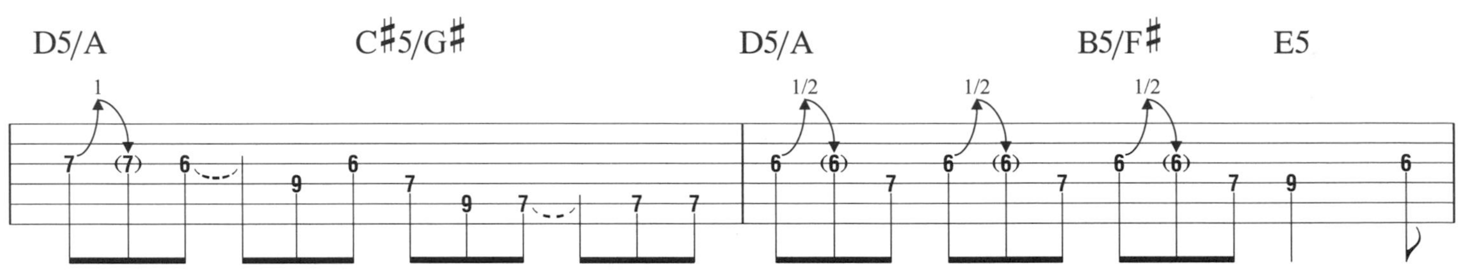

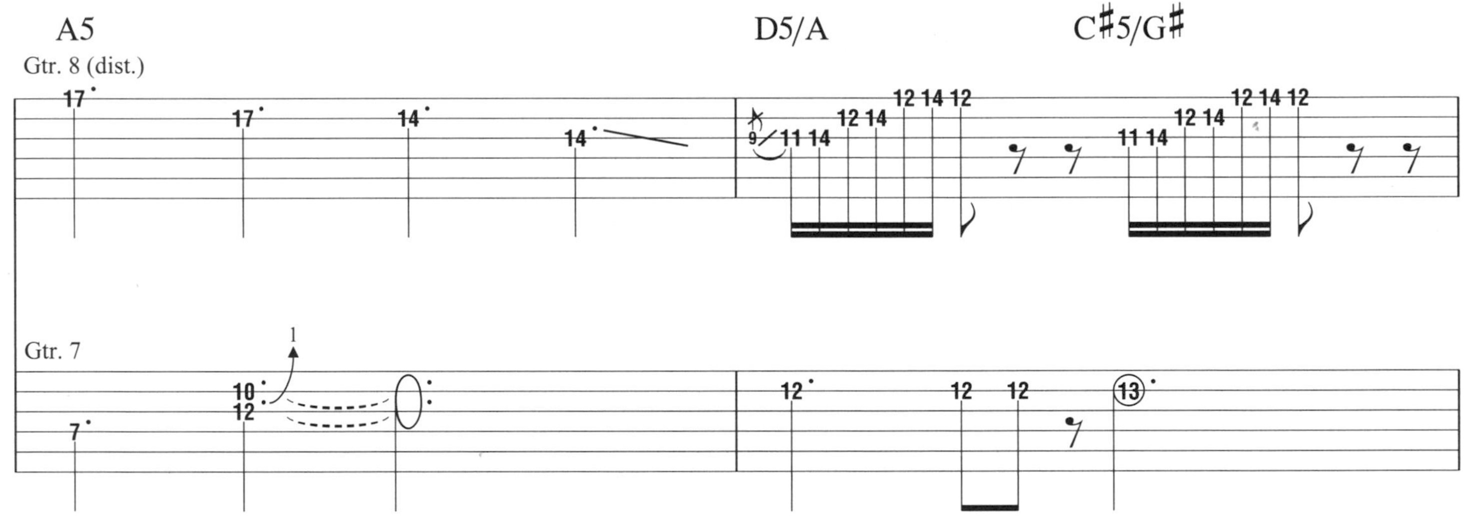

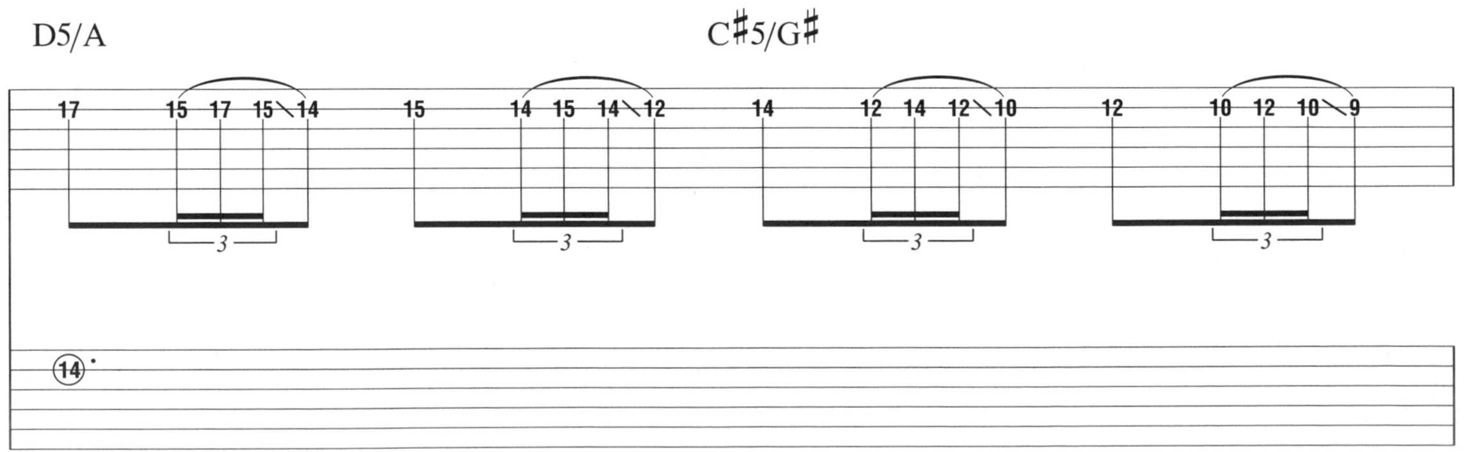

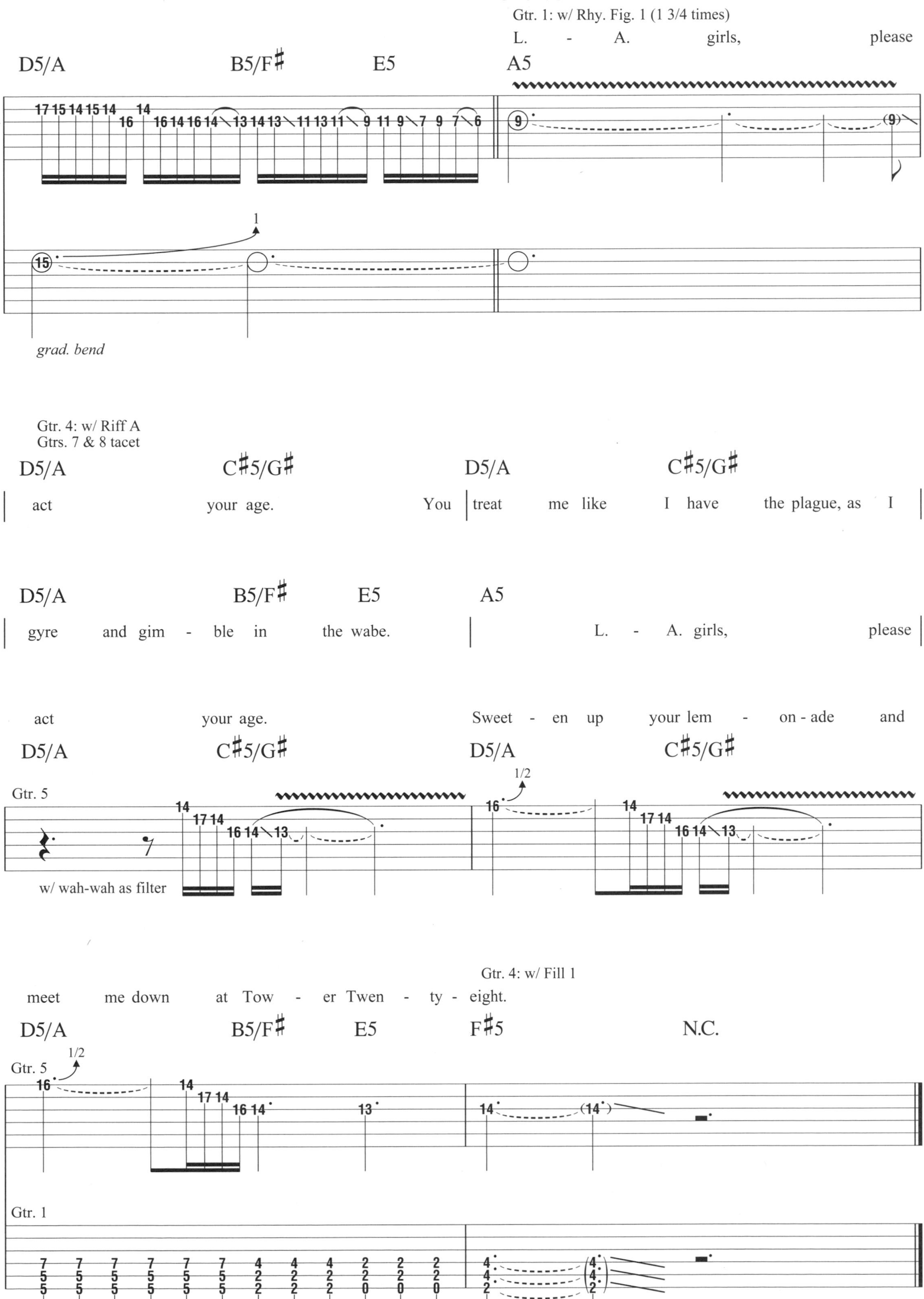
Chorus
Gtr. 1: w/ Rhy. Fig. 1 (1 3/4 times)
L. - A. girls, please
D5/A
B5/F#
E5
A5
grad. bend
Gtr. 4: w/ Riff A
Gtrs. 7 & 8 tacet
D5/A
C#5/G#
act your age. You
treat me like I have the plague, as I
gyre and gim - ble in the wabe.
L. - A. girls, please
act your age.
Sweet - en up your lem - on - ade and
Gtr. 5
w/ wah-wah as filter
meet me down at Tow - er Twen - ty - eight.
Gtr. 4: w/ Fill 1
F#5
N.C.
Gtr. 1

Jacked Up

Words and Music by Rivers Cuomo, Jonathan Coffer and Hugh Pescod

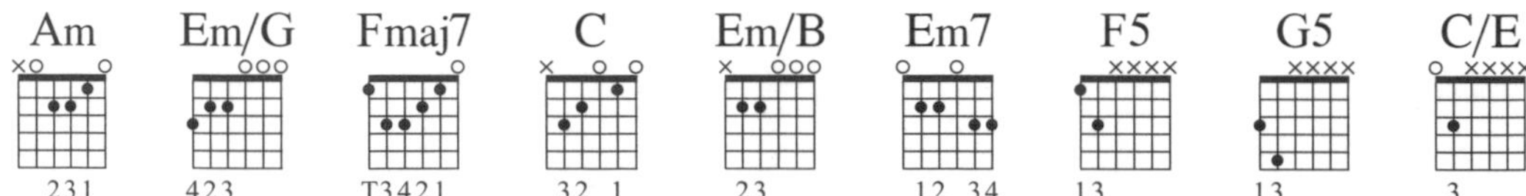

Tune down 1/4 step

Key of Am

Intro

Moderately slow ♩ = 91

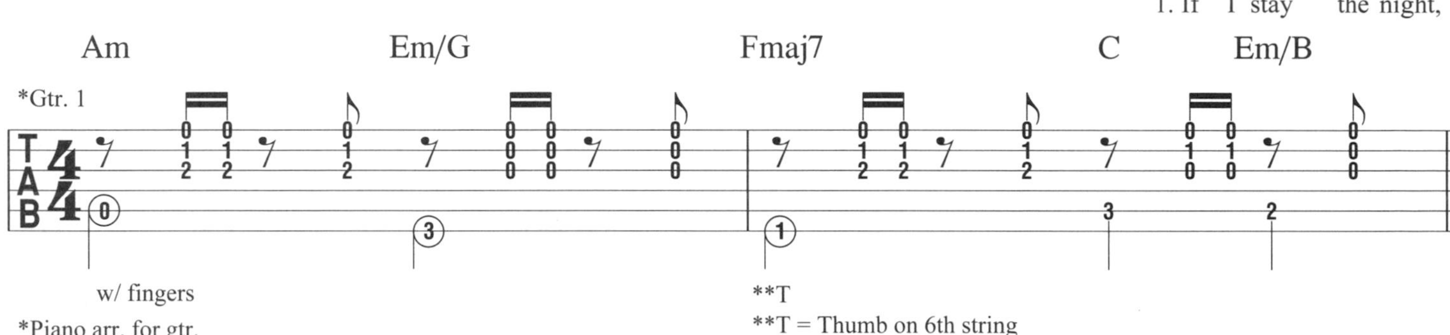

*Piano arr. for gtr.

**T = Thumb on 6th string

Verse

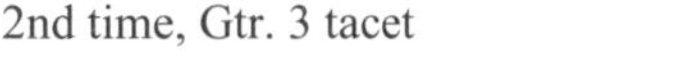

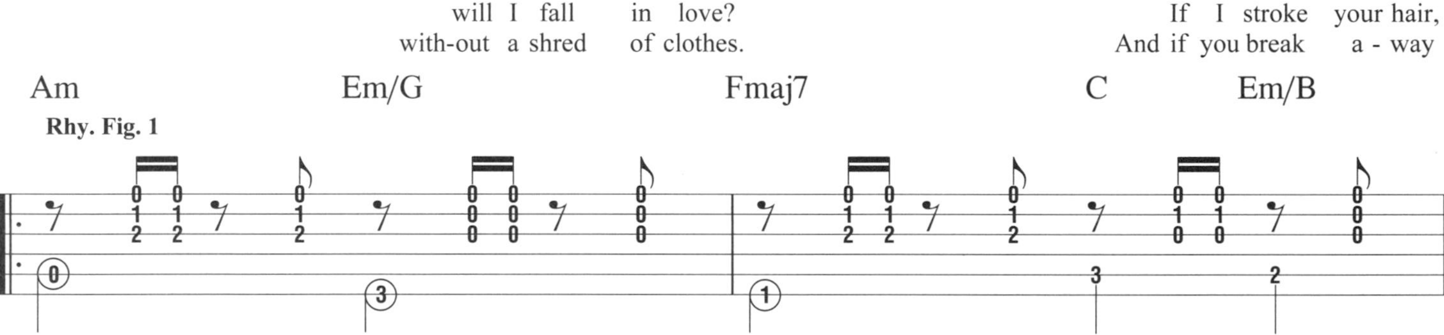

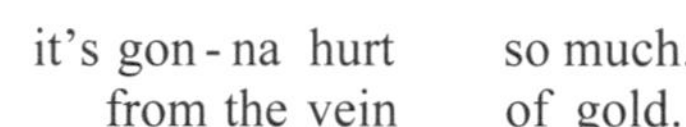

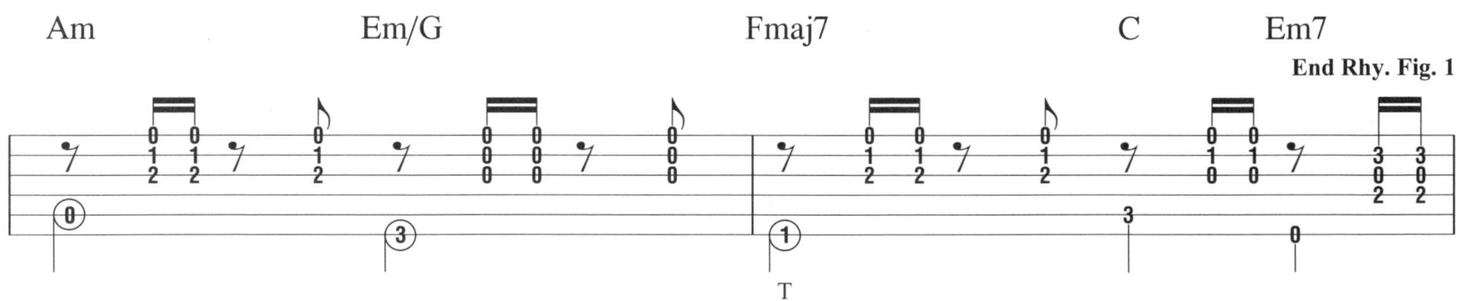

Gtr. 1: w/ Rhy. Fig. 1

Am Em/G Fmaj7 C Em/B

Strand - ed in the Kal - a - har - i, will you share your flask? If } I stay the night,
Come, my beau - ti - ful al - i - en, touch me with your light. But if }

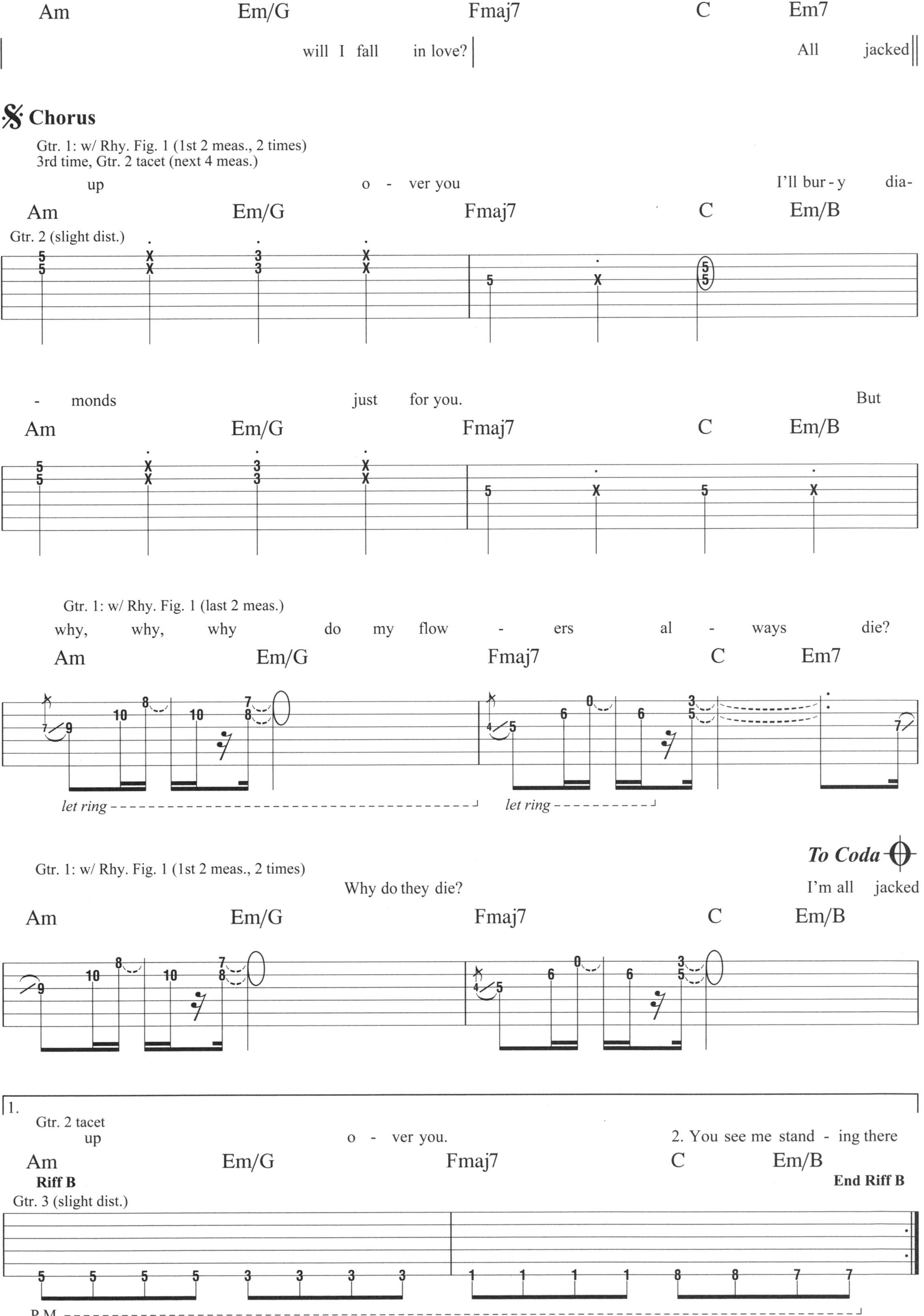

Am
Em/G
Fmaj7
C
Em7
will I fall in love?
All jacked
Chorus
Gtr. 1: w/ Rhy. Fig. 1 (1st 2 meas., 2 times)
3rd time, Gtr. 2 tacet (next 4 meas.)
up o - ver you
I'll bur - y dia-
Em/B
Gtr. 2 (slight dist.)
- monds just for you.
But
Gtr. 1: w/ Rhy. Fig. 1 (last 2 meas.)
why, why, why do my flow - ers al - ways die?
let ring
Gtr. 1: w/ Rhy. Fig. 1 (1st 2 meas., 2 times)
Why do they die?
To Coda
I'm all jacked
1.
Gtr. 2 tacet
up o - ver you.
2. You see me stand - ing there
Riff B
End Riff B
Gtr. 3 (slight dist.)
P.M.

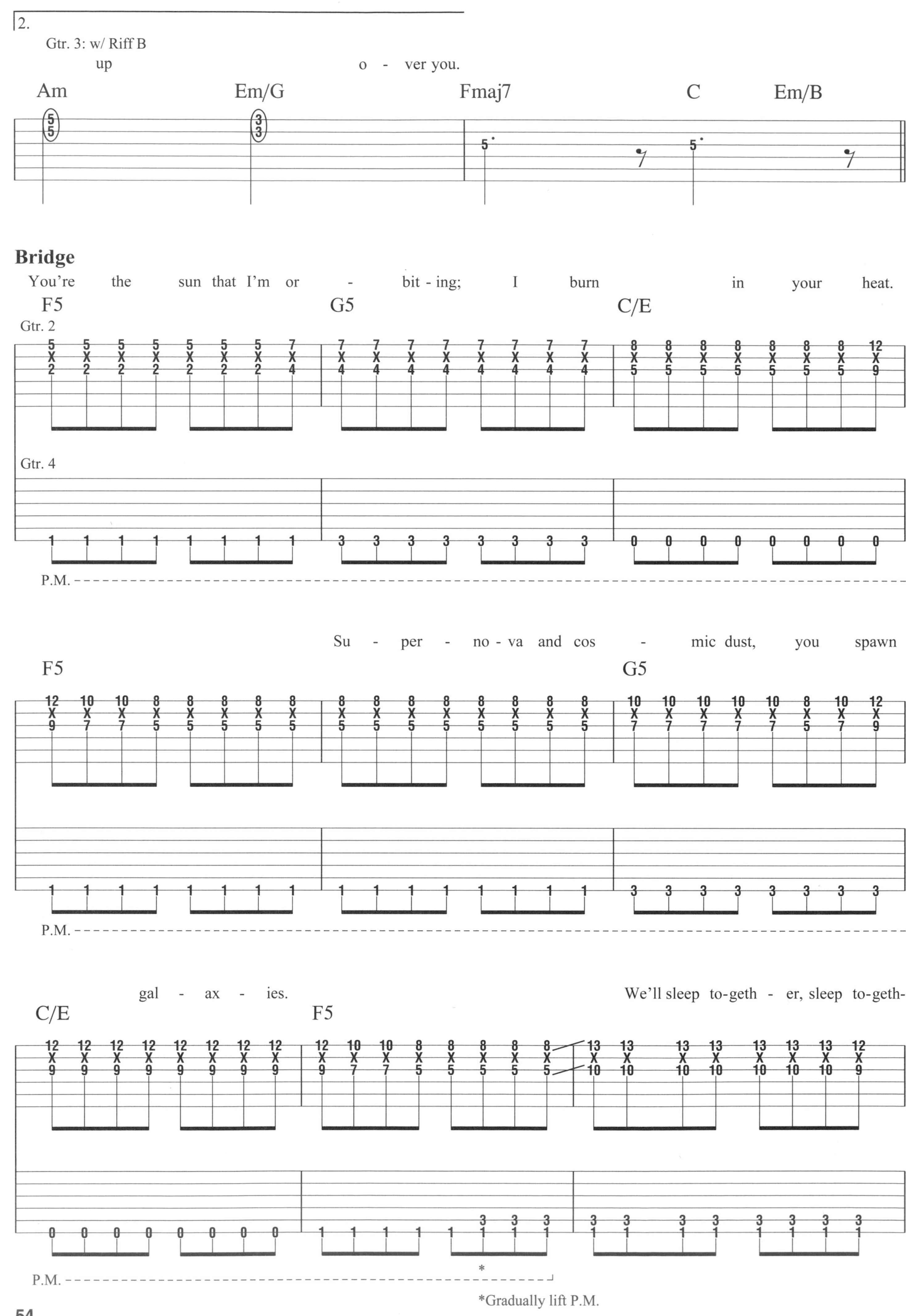
2.
Gtr. 3: w/ Riff B
up o - ver you.
Am
Em/G
Fmaj7
C
Em/B
Bridge
You're the sun that I'm or - bit - ing; I burn in your heat.
F5
G5
C/E
Gtr. 2
Gtr. 4
P.M.
Su - per - no - va and cos - mic dust, you spawn
F5
G5
P.M.
gal - ax - ies. We'll sleep to-geth - er, sleep to-geth-
C/E
F5
P.M.
*Gradually lift P.M.

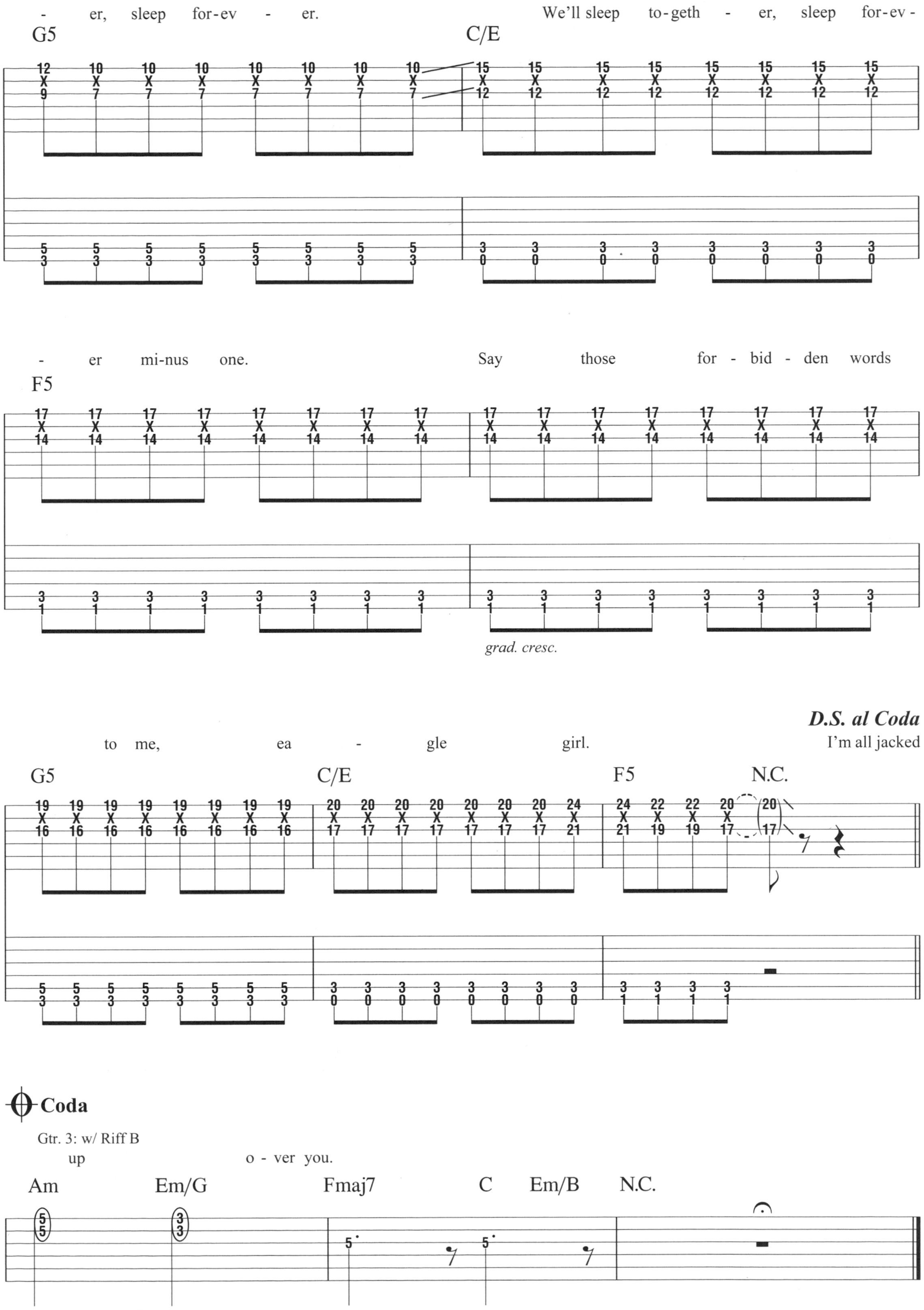

- er, sleep for-ev - er. We'll sleep to-geth - er, sleep for-ev -

G5 C/E

- er mi-nus one. Say those for - bid - den words

F5

grad. cresc.

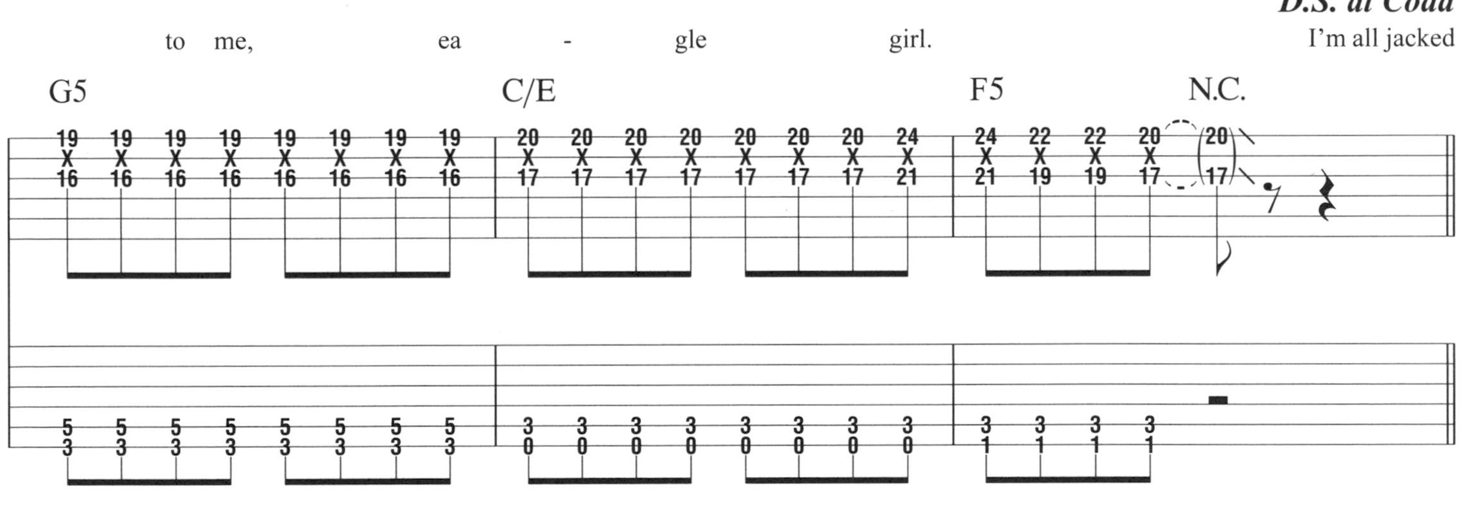

Coda

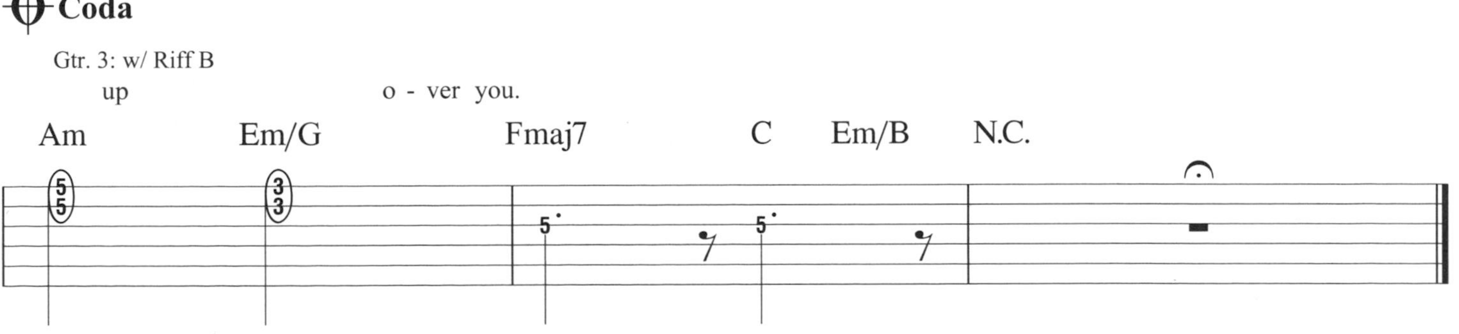

Endless Bummer

Words and Music by Rivers Cuomo, Brian Bell and Luther Russell

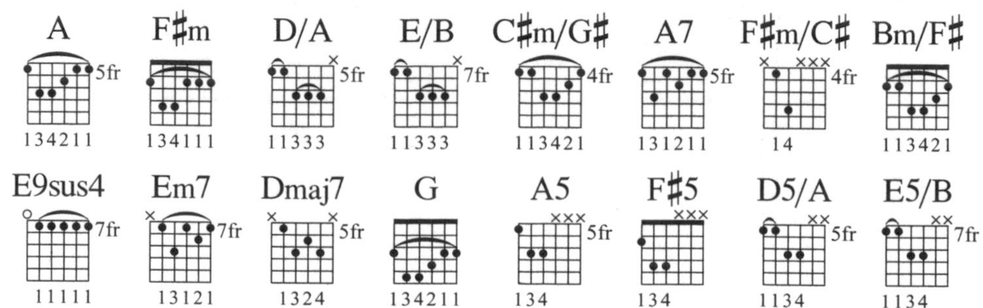

Tune down 1/2 step:
(low to high) E♭-A♭-D♭-G♭-B♭-E♭

Key of A

Intro

Moderately ♩ = 108

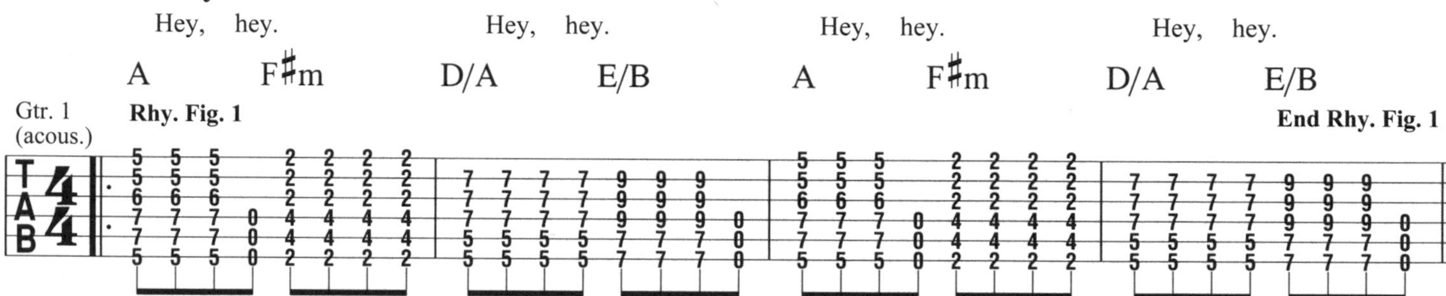

Verse

Gtr. 1: w/ Rhy. Fig. 1 (4 times)

A F♯m D/A E/B A F♯m D/A E/B

1. I just want the sum - mer to end.
2. No life from Pa - lo - ma to Rose.

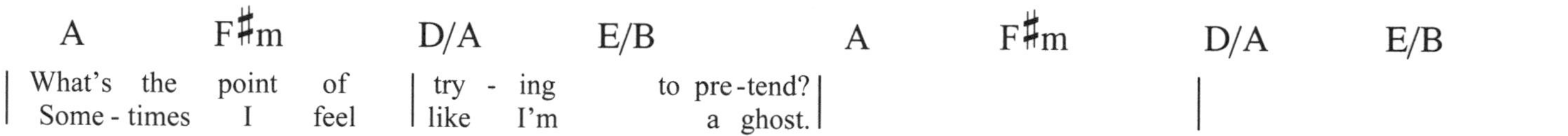

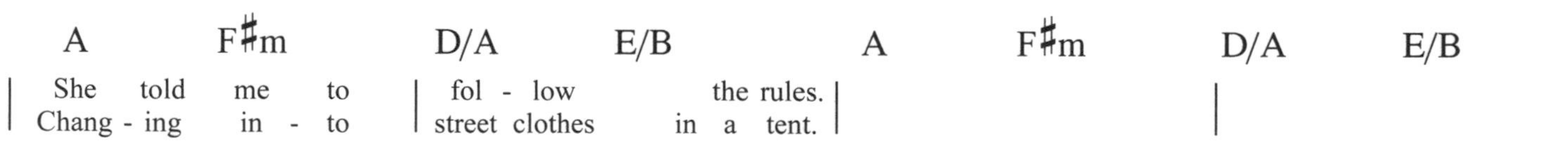

A F♯m D/A E/B A F♯m D/A E/B

Not all nine - teen - year - olds are cool.
I just want the sum - mer to end. (Sum - mer to end.)

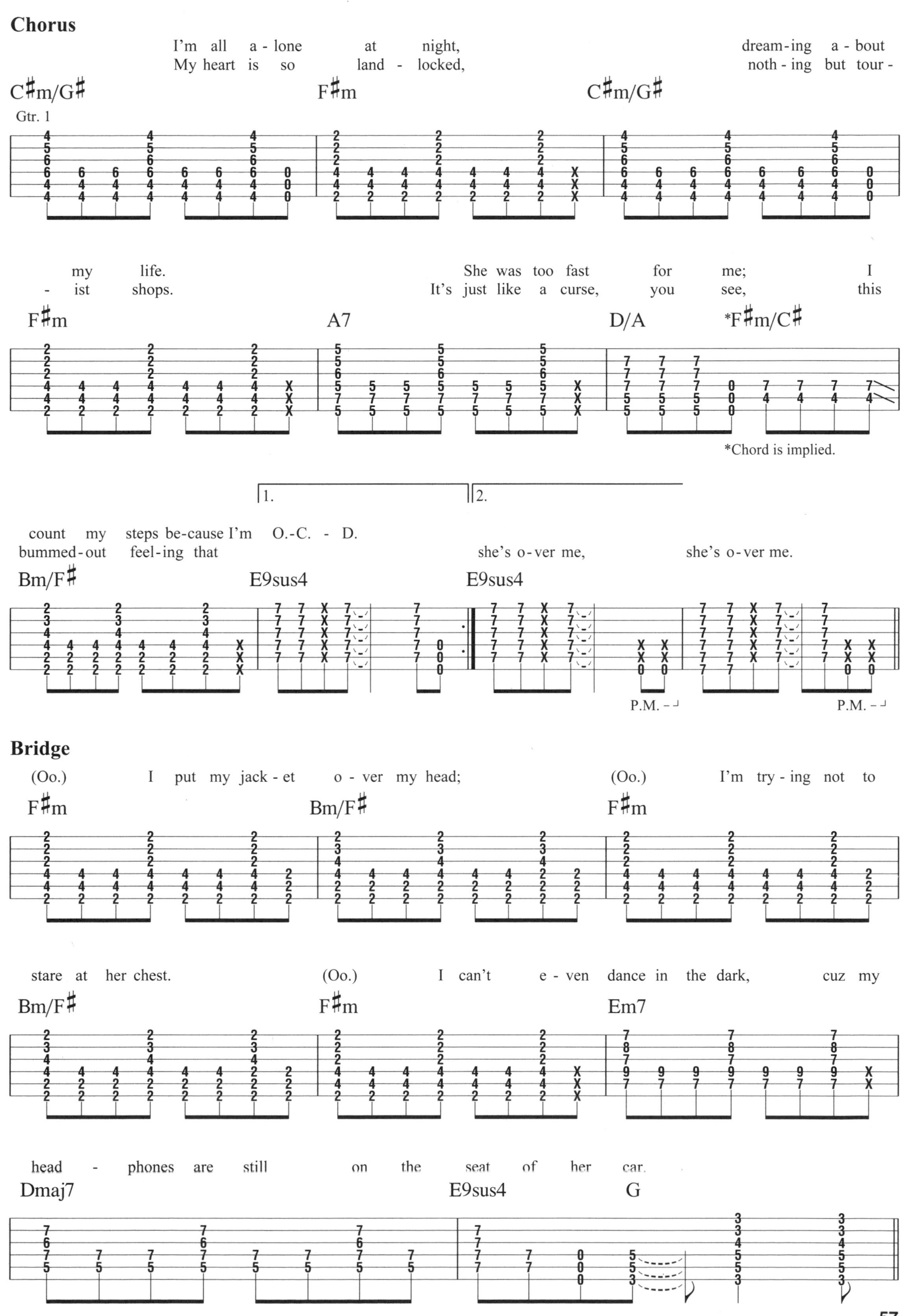
Chorus
I'm all a - lone at night, dream-ing a - bout
My heart is so land - locked, noth - ing but tour -
C♯m/G♯
F♯m
C♯m/G♯
Gtr. 1
my life. She was too fast for me; I
- ist shops. It's just like a curse, you see, this
F♯m
A7
D/A
*F♯m/C♯
*Chord is implied.
1.
2.
count my steps be-cause I'm O.-C. - D.
bummed-out feel-ing that she's o-ver me, she's o-ver me.
Bm/F♯
E9sus4
E9sus4
P.M.
P.M.
Bridge
(Oo.) I put my jack - et o - ver my head; (Oo.) I'm try - ing not to
F♯m
Bm/F♯
F♯m
stare at her chest. (Oo.) I can't e - ven dance in the dark, cuz my
Bm/F♯
F♯m
Em7
head - phones are still on the seat of her car.
Dmaj7
E9sus4
G

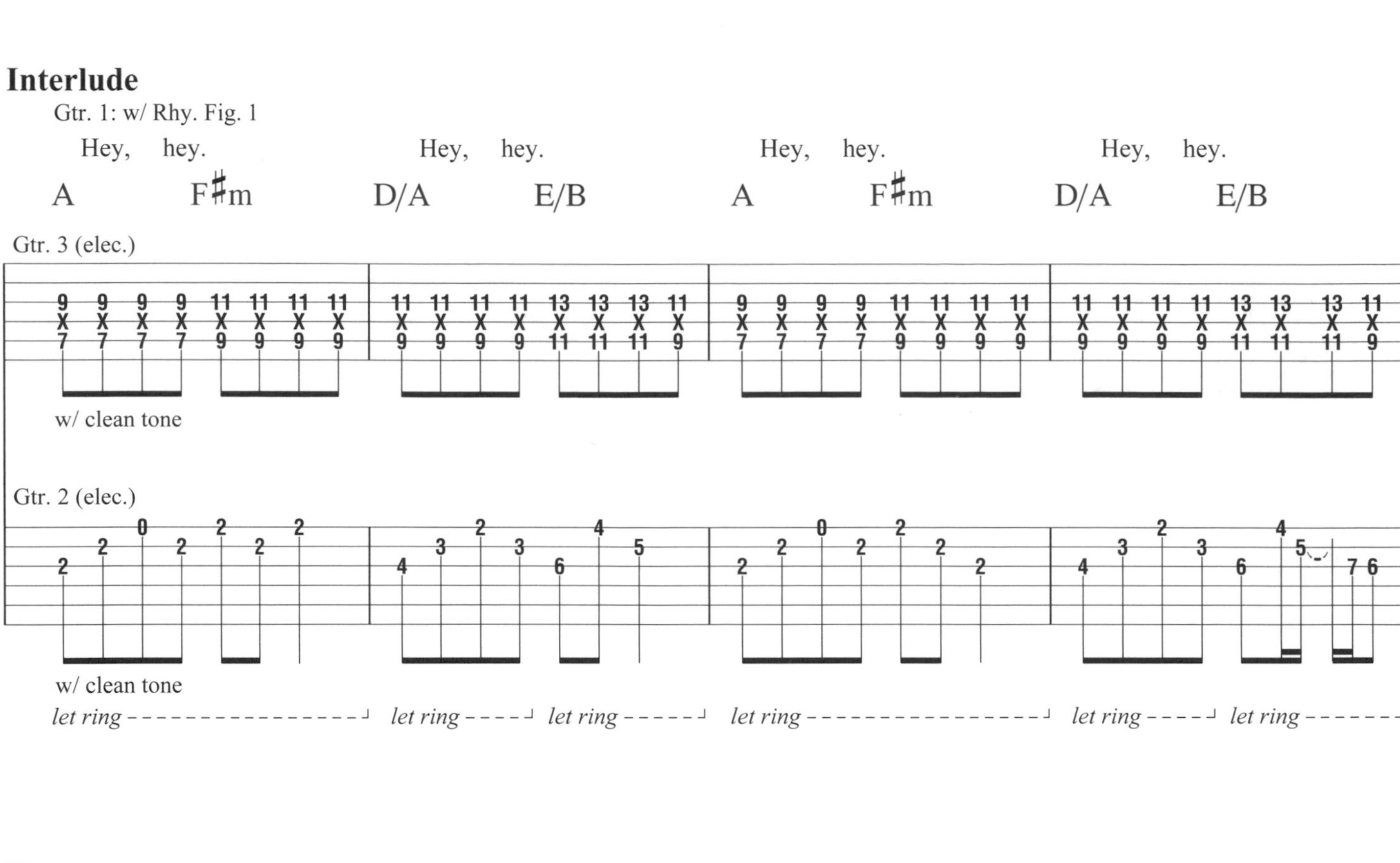
Interlude
Gtr. 1: w/ Rhy. Fig. 1
Hey, hey. Hey, hey. Hey, hey. Hey, hey.
A F♯m D/A E/B A F♯m D/A E/B
Gtr. 3 (elec.)
w/ clean tone
Gtr. 2 (elec.)
w/ clean tone
let ring let ring let ring let ring let ring let ring

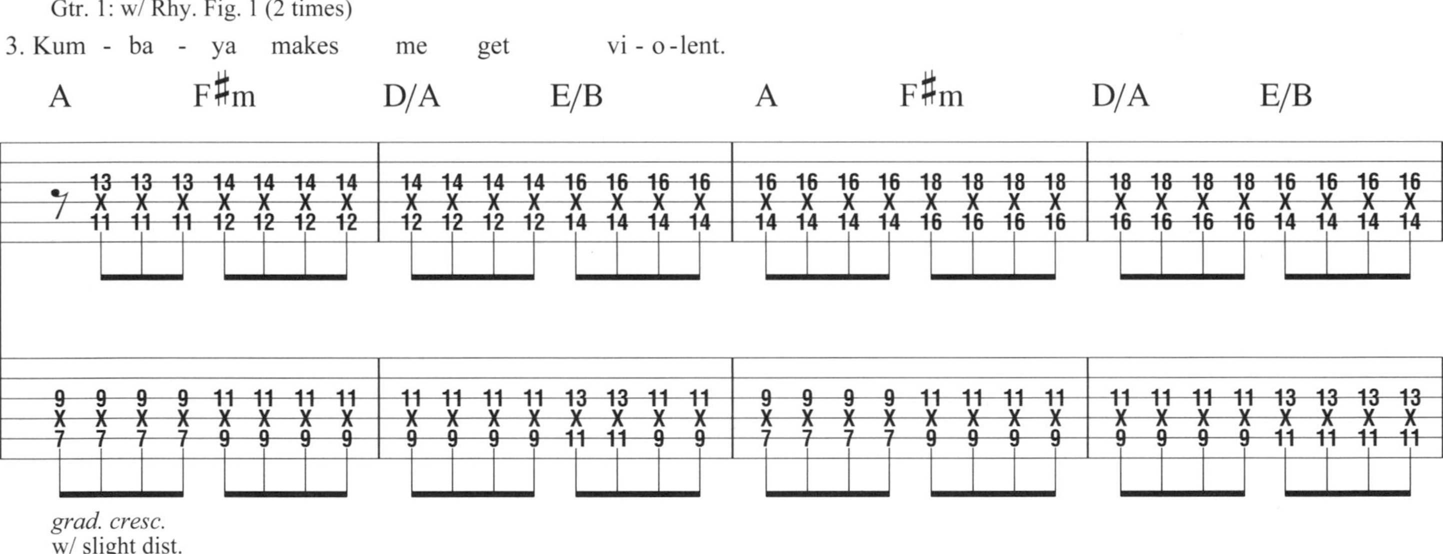
Verse
Gtr. 1: w/ Rhy. Fig. 1 (2 times)
3. Kum - ba - ya makes me get vi - o - lent.
A F♯m D/A E/B A F♯m D/A E/B
grad. cresc.
w/ slight dist.

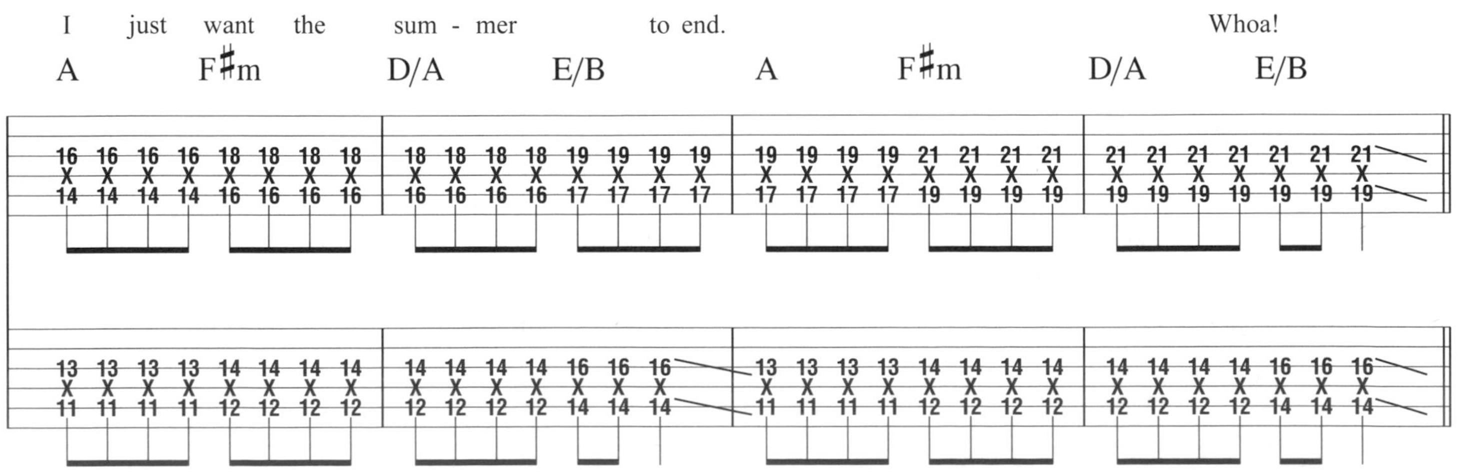
I just want the sum - mer to end. Whoa!
A F♯m D/A E/B A F♯m D/A E/B

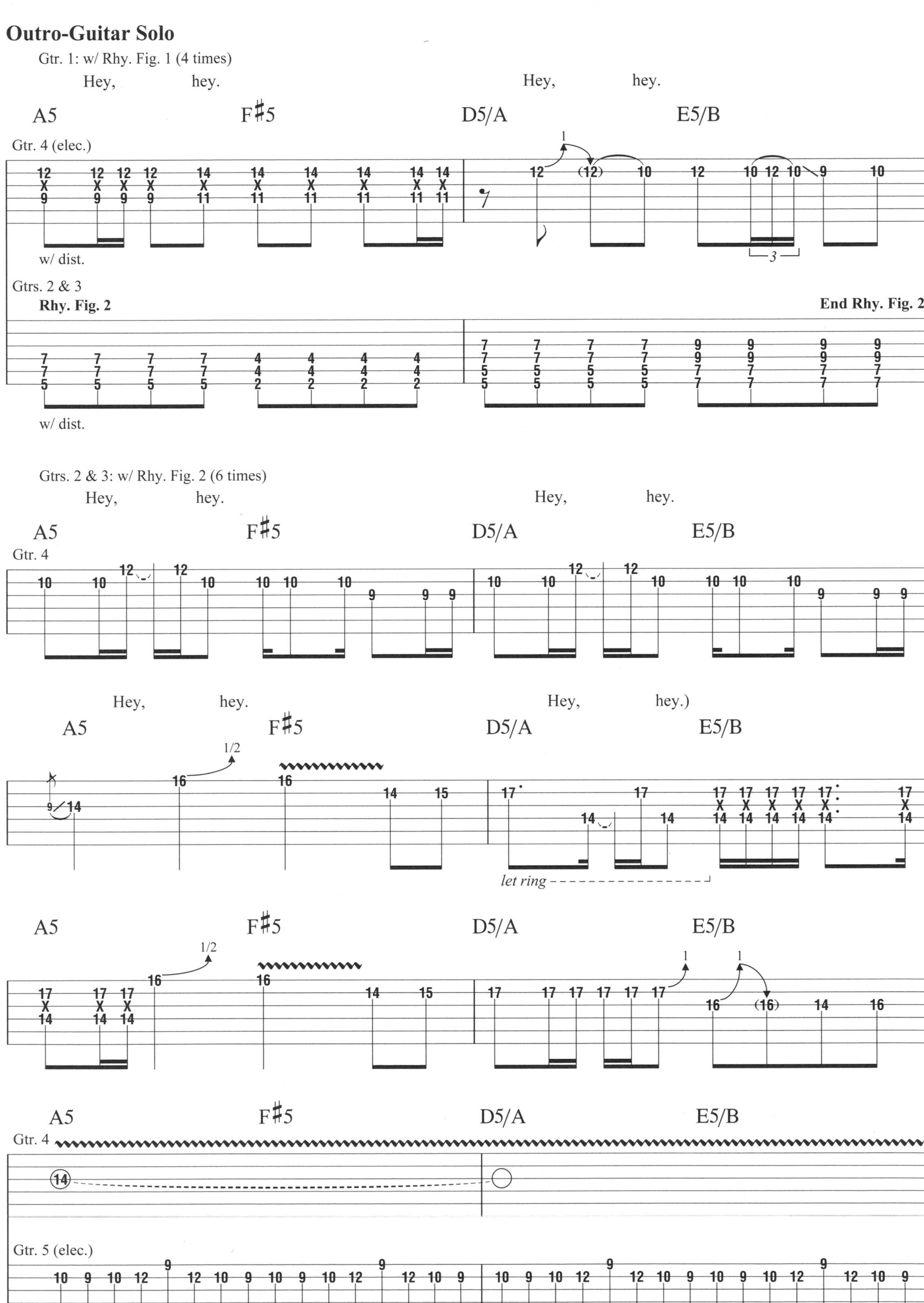
Outro-Guitar Solo
Gtr. 1: w/ Rhy. Fig. 1 (4 times)
Hey, hey. Hey, hey.
A5 F♯5 D5/A E5/B
Gtr. 4 (elec.)
w/ dist.
Gtrs. 2 & 3
Rhy. Fig. 2
End Rhy. Fig. 2
w/ dist.
Gtrs. 2 & 3: w/ Rhy. Fig. 2 (6 times)
Hey, hey. Hey, hey.
A5 F♯5 D5/A E5/B
Gtr. 4
Hey, hey. Hey, hey.)
A5 F♯5 D5/A E5/B
let ring
A5 F♯5 D5/A E5/B
A5 F♯5 D5/A E5/B
Gtr. 4
Gtr. 5 (elec.)
w/ dist.

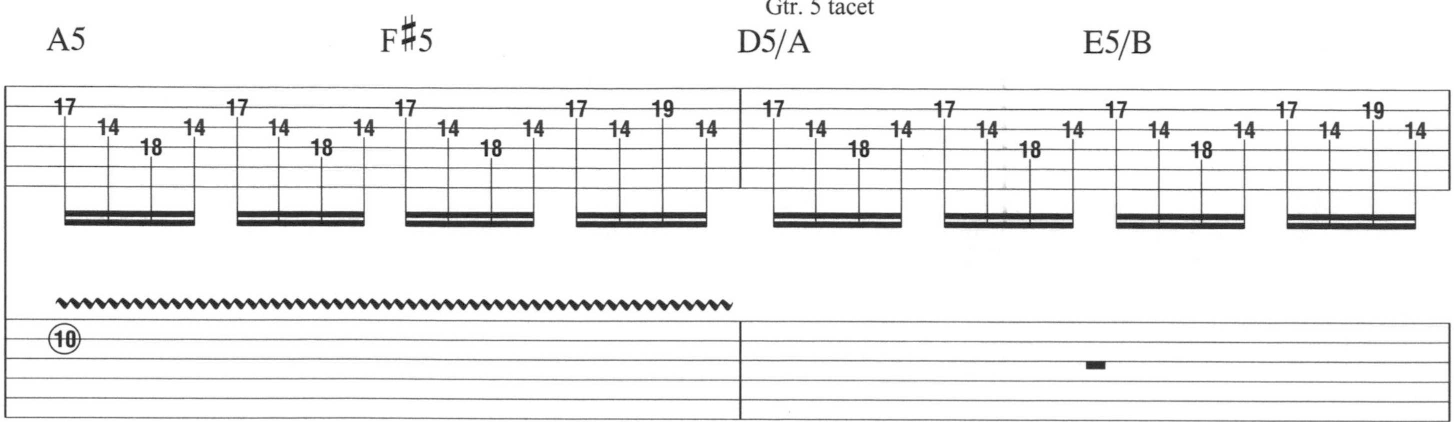
Gtr. 5 tacet
A5
F♯5
D5/A
E5/B

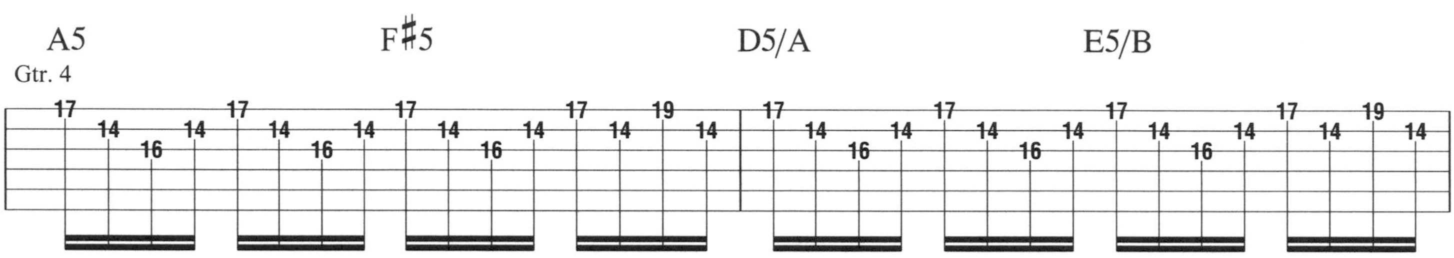
A5
F♯5
D5/A
E5/B
Gtr. 4

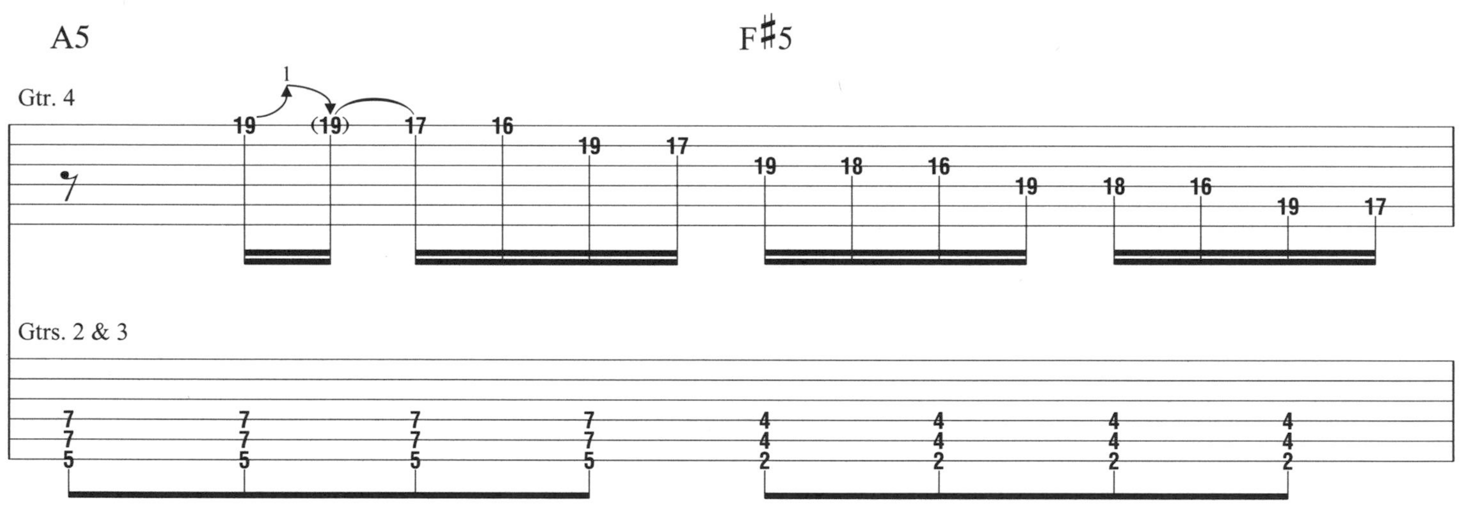
A5
F♯5
Gtr. 4
Gtrs. 2 & 3

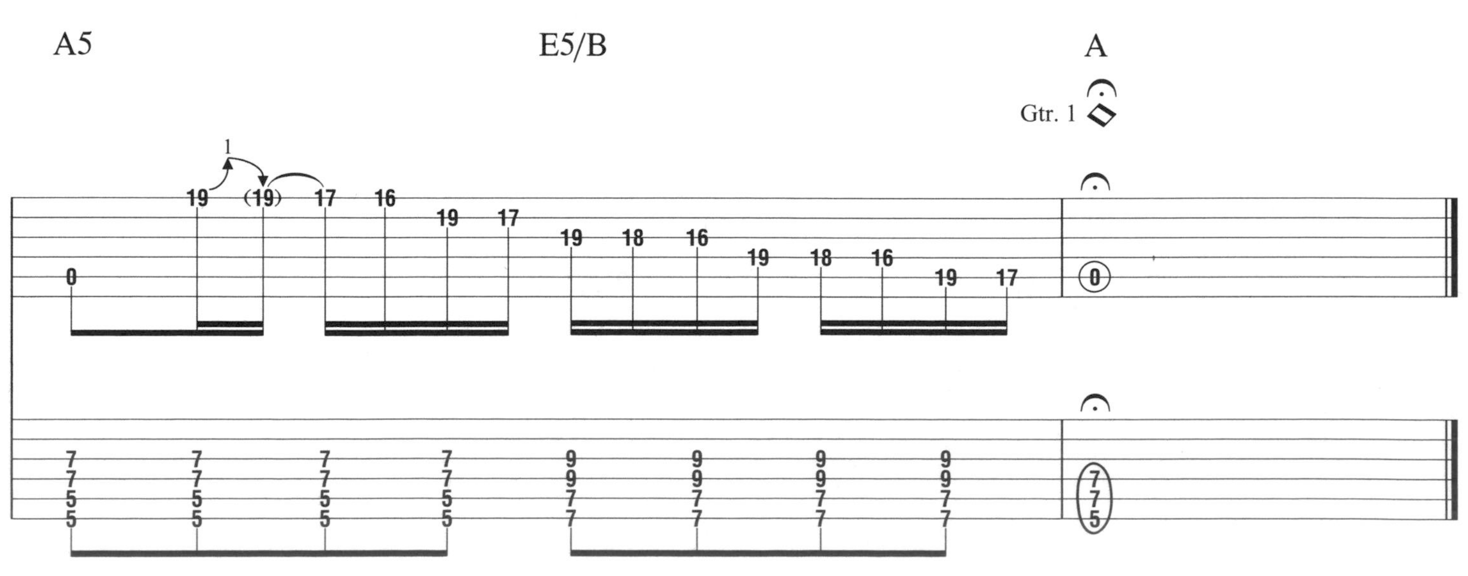
A5
E5/B
A
Gtr. 1

RHYTHM TAB LEGEND

Rhythm Tab is a form of notation that adds rhythmic values to the traditional tab staff.

TABLATURE graphically represents the guitar fingerboard. Each horizontal line represents a string, and each number represents a fret. Rhythmic values are shown using ovals, stems, and dots.

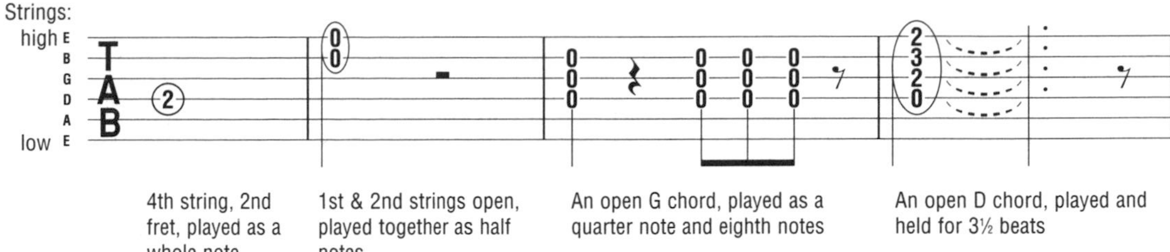

4th string, 2nd fret, played as a whole note

1st & 2nd strings open, played together as half notes

An open G chord, played as a quarter note and eighth notes

An open D chord, played and held for 3½ beats

Definitions for Special Guitar Notation

HALF-STEP BEND: Strike the note and bend up 1/2 step.

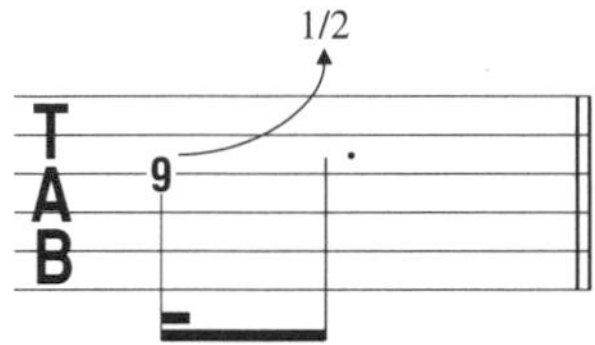

WHOLE-STEP BEND: Strike the note and bend up one step.

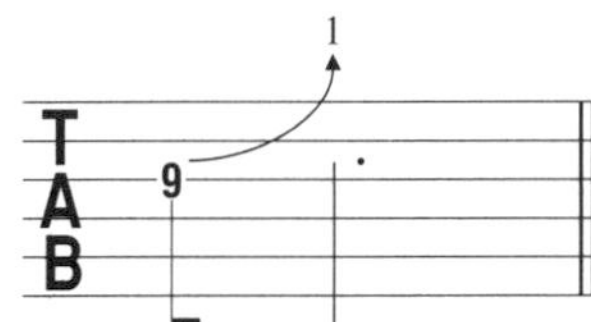

GRACE NOTE BEND: Strike the note and immediately bend up as indicated.

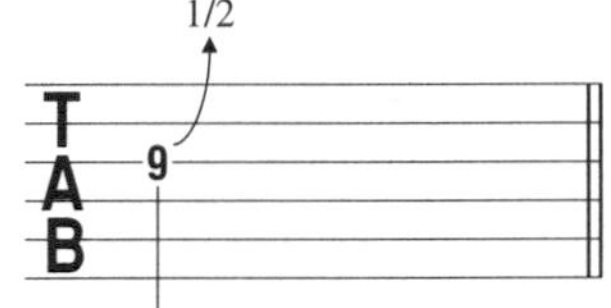

SLIGHT (MICROTONE) BEND: Strike the note and bend up 1/4 step.

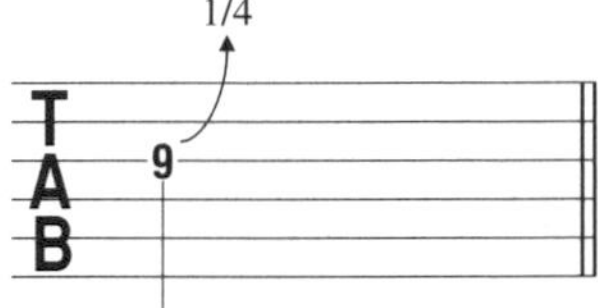

BEND AND RELEASE: Strike the note and bend up as indicated, then release back to the original note. Only the first note is struck.

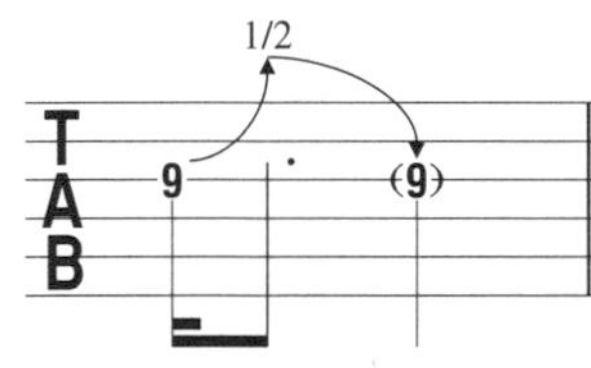

PRE-BEND: Bend the note as indicated, then strike it.

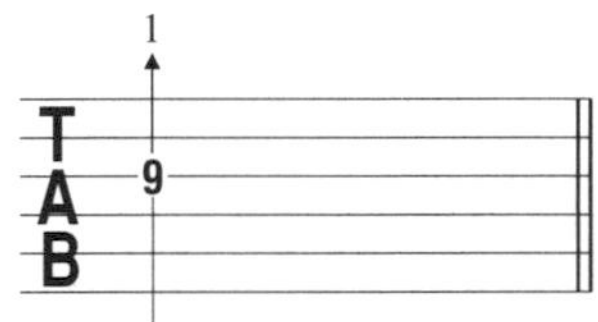

PRE-BEND AND RELEASE: Bend the note as indicated. Strike it and release the bend back to the original note.

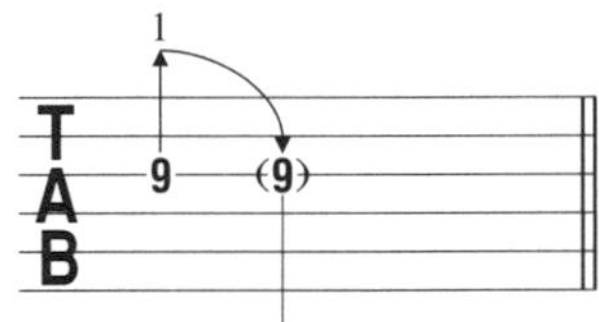

UNISON BEND: Strike the two notes simultaneously and bend the lower note up to the pitch of the higher.

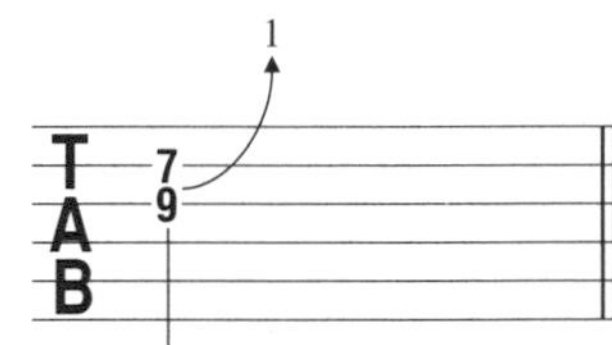

HOLD BEND: While sustaining bent note, strike note on different string.

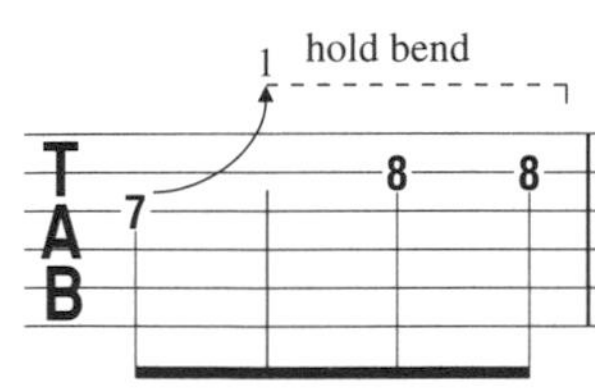

VIBRATO: The string is vibrated by rapidly bending and releasing the note with the fretting hand.

WIDE VIBRATO: The pitch is varied to a greater degree by vibrating with the fretting hand.

HAMMER-ON: Strike the first (lower) note with one finger, then sound the higher note (on the same string) with another finger by fretting it without picking.

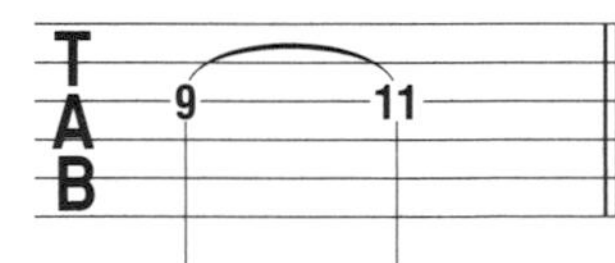

PULL-OFF: Place both fingers on the notes to be sounded. Strike the first note and without picking, pull the finger off to sound the second (lower) note.

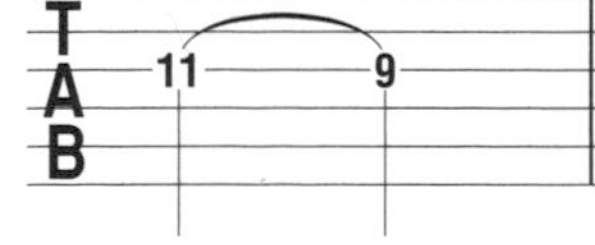

HAMMER FROM NOWHERE: Sound note(s) by hammering with fret hand finger only.

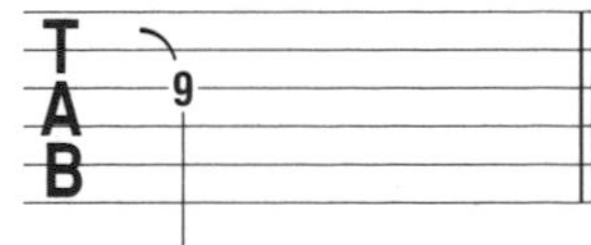

GRACE NOTE SLUR: Strike the note and immediately hammer-on (or pull-off) as indicated.

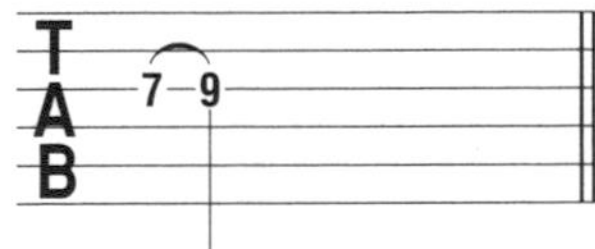

GRACE NOTE SLUR (CLUSTER): Strike the notes and immediately hammer-on (or pull-off) as indicated.

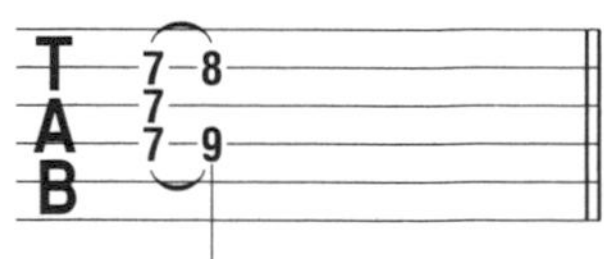

LEGATO SLIDE: Strike the first note and then slide the same fret-hand finger up or down to the second note. The second note is not struck.

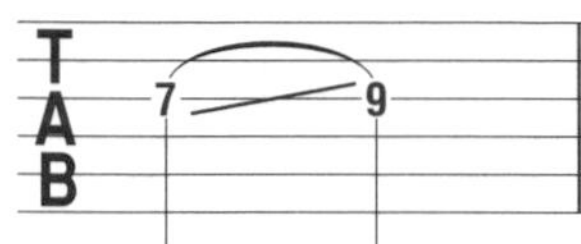

SHIFT SLIDE: Same as legato slide, except the second note is struck.

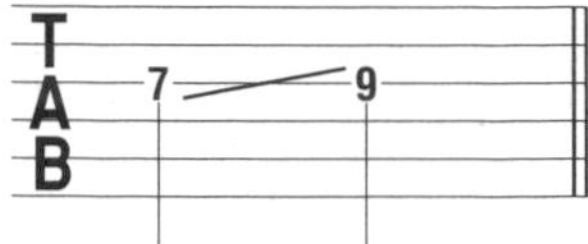

TRILL: Very rapidly alternate between the notes indicated by continuously hammering on and pulling off.

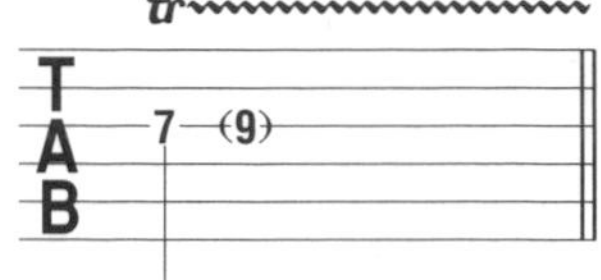

TAPPING: Hammer ("tap") the fret indicated with the pick-hand index or middle finger and pull off to the note fretted by the fret hand.

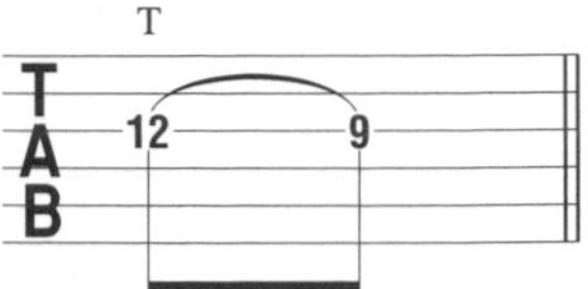

NATURAL HARMONIC: Strike the note while the fret-hand lightly touches the string directly over the fret indicated.

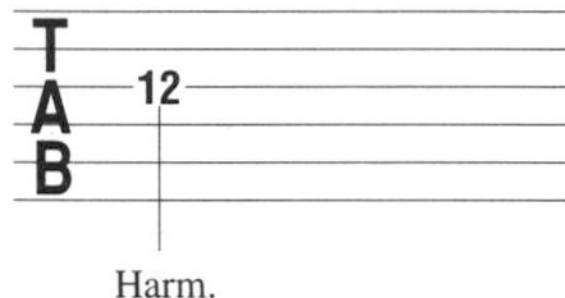

PINCH HARMONIC: The note is fretted normally and a harmonic is produced by adding the edge of the thumb or the tip of the index finger of the pick hand to the normal pick attack.

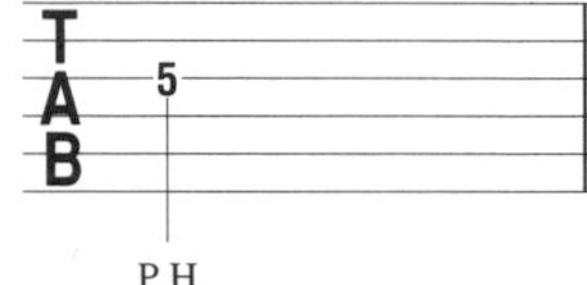

HARP HARMONIC: The note is fretted normally and a harmonic is produced by gently resting the pick hand's index finger directly above the indicated fret (in parentheses) while the pick hand's thumb or pick assists by plucking the appropriate string.

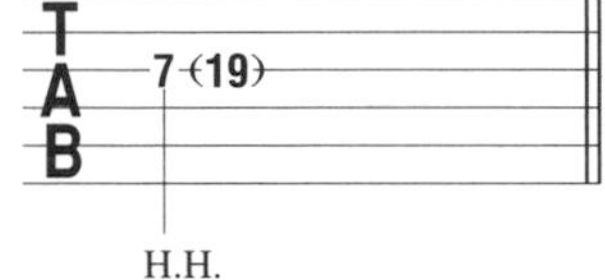

PICK SCRAPE: The edge of the pick is rubbed down (or up) the string, producing a scratchy sound.

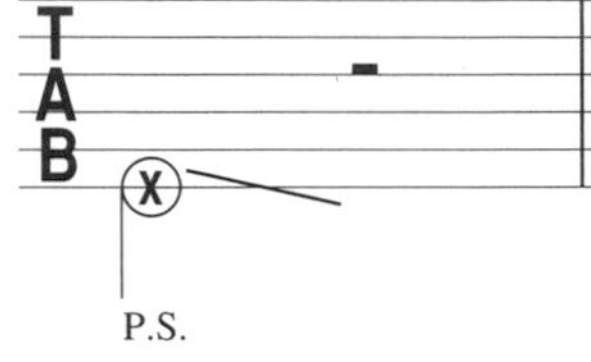

MUFFLED STRINGS: A percussive sound is produced by laying the fret hand across the string(s) without depressing, and striking them with the pick hand.

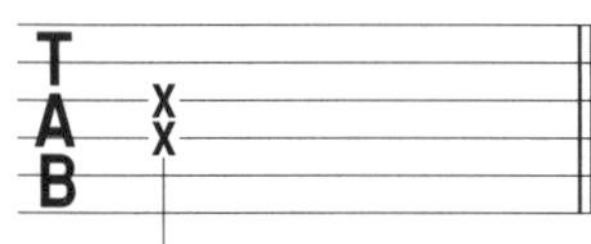

PALM MUTING: The note is partially muted by the pick hand lightly touching the string(s) just before the bridge.

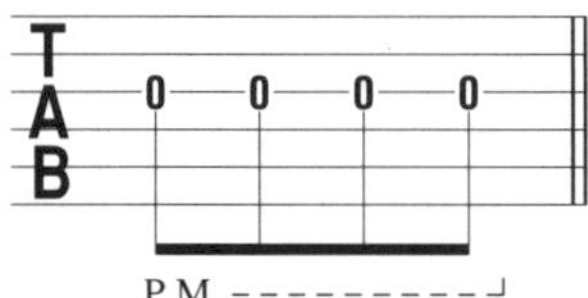

RAKE: Drag the pick across the strings indicated with a single motion.

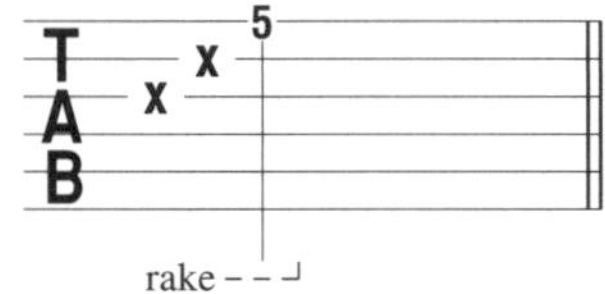

TREMOLO PICKING: The note is picked as rapidly and continuously as possible.

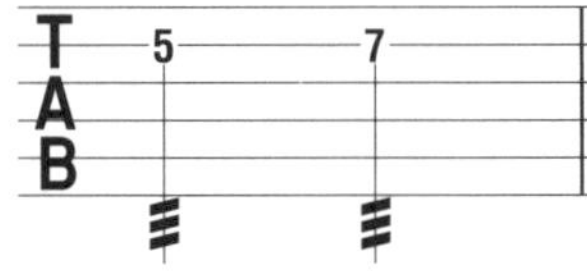

ARPEGGIATE: Play the notes of the chord indicated by quickly rolling them from bottom to top.

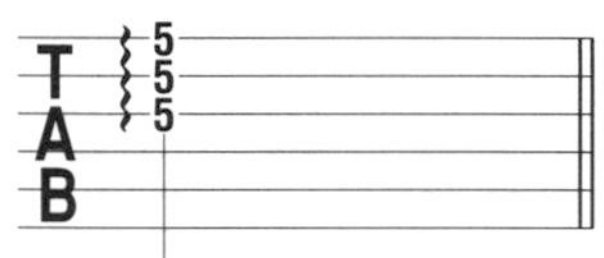

VIBRATO BAR DIVE AND RETURN: The pitch of the note or chord is dropped a specified number of steps (in rhythm), then returned to the original pitch.

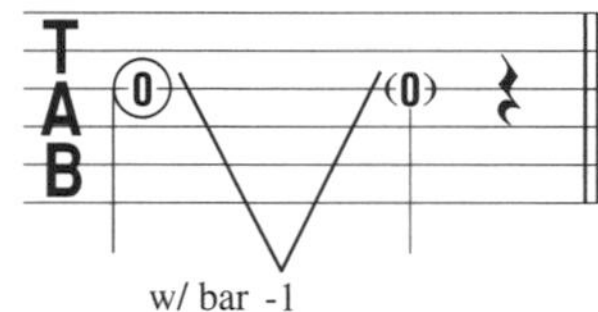

VIBRATO BAR SCOOP: Depress the bar just before striking the note, then quickly release the bar.

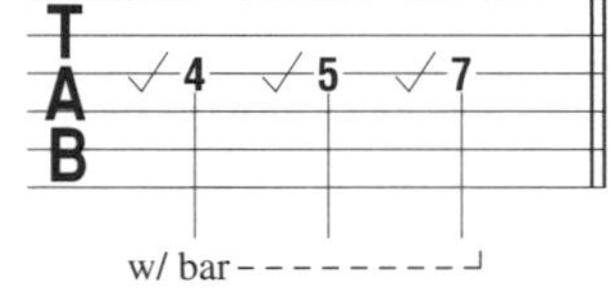

VIBRATO BAR DIP: Strike the note and then immediately drop a specified number of steps, then release back to the original pitch.

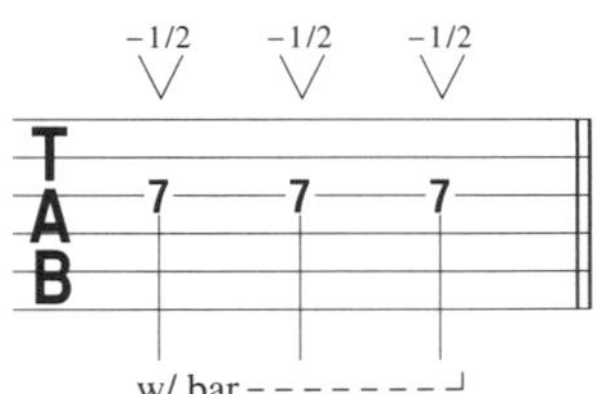

Additional Musical Definitions

3 *(accent)* • Accentuate note (play it louder)

3 *(staccato)* • Play the note short

3 *(fermata)* • A hold or pause

• Downstroke

V • Upstroke

• Repeat measures between signs

NOTE: Tablature numbers in parentheses are used when:

- The note is sustained, but a new articulation begins (such as a hammer-on, pull-off, slide, or bend), or
- A bend is released.

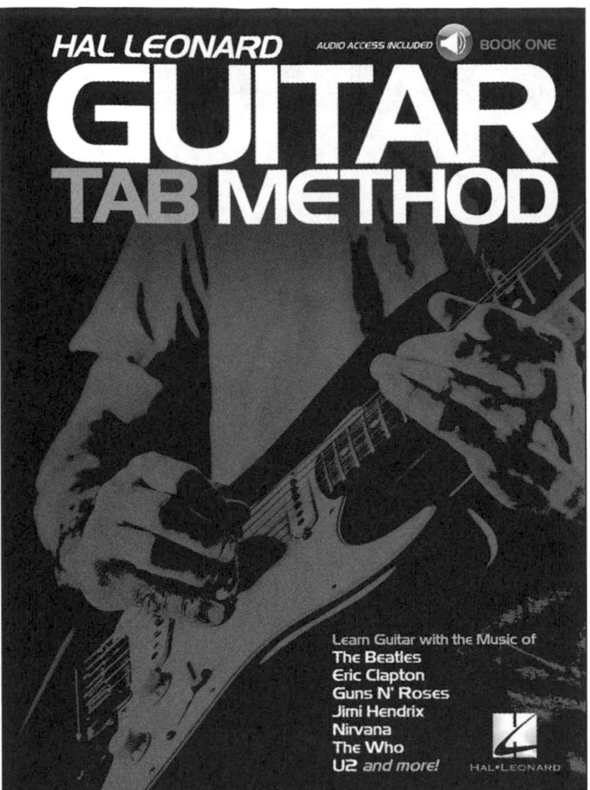

HAL LEONARD GUITAR TAB METHOD

THE FIRST AND ONLY BEGINNING GUITAR METHOD OF ITS KIND!

HAL LEONARD GUITAR TAB METHOD

Learn single notes with riffs like "Day Tripper" and "Crazy Train," power chords with classics by AC/DC and the Who, strumming with songs from Neil Young and Nirvana, and much more. Book 1 includes: parts of the guitar, easy-to-follow guitar tablature, notes & riffs starting on the low E string, tempo & time signatures, understanding notes and rests, palm muting, vibrato, power chords, open chords, strumming, slides and slurs, hammer-ons and pull-offs, many music styles, nearly 100 riffs and songs, online audio demos of every example, and more!

00697411 Book/Online Audio $12.99

BOOK 2

This innovative method for acoustic or electric guitar picks up where Book One leaves off. Learn notes up the fretboard with riffs like "Purple Haze" and "Sunshine of Your Love," lead guitar licks from Stevie Ray Vaughan and Eric Clapton, more chords with songs by the Beatles and Bob Dylan, and much more. The accompanying online audio access, available using the unique code in the book, features demos of all 80 riffs and songs in the book.

00696616 Book/Online Audio $12.99

BOOKS 1 & 2 COMBO EDITION

00696633 Book/Online Audio $24.99

BOOK 3

Book 3 includes: easy-to-follow guitar tablature; barre chords; minor scale; relative minor; Nashville numbering system; 12-bar blues; blues scale; blues licks & turnarounds; 12/8 time; add and sus chords; minor seventh chords; minor blues; variety of music styles; nearly 80 riffs and songs; audio demos of every example; and much more.

00126952 Book/Online Audio $12.99

SONGBOOK 1

Here are 10 hit songs tabbed for beginning guitarists to play while they are working through the Hal Leonard Guitar Tab Method, or any other guitar method. The CD features both examples of how the guitar should sound, and full-band backing tracks so students can play the lead! Songs: All the Small Things • Breaking the Law • Californication • Come Together • Free Fallin' • Lick It Up • Pork and Beans • Smells like Teen Spirit • 21 Guns • You Really Got Me.

00696604 Book/CD Pack $12.99

SONGBOOK 2

Here are 10 more hit songs to play while working through the Hal Leonard Guitar Tab Method: Born under a Bad Sign • Brain Stew • Fortunate Son • I Won't Back Down • Lithium • Mr. Jones • Rebel 'Rouser • Rolling in the Deep • Use Somebody • The Zoo.

00696655 Book/CD Pack $12.99

HAL LEONARD ACOUSTIC GUITAR TAB METHOD BOOK 1

Learn chords with songs like "Eleanor Rigby" and "Knockin' on Heaven's Door," single notes with riffs and solos by Nirvana and Pink Floyd, arpeggios with classics by Eric Clapton and Boston, and much more. Book 1 includes: parts of the guitar, easy-to-follow guitar tablature, notes & riffs starting on the low E string, tempo & time signatures, strumming patterns and arpeggios, slides and slurs, hammer-ons and pull-offs, many music styles, nearly 100 riffs and songs, audio demos of every example, and more!

00124197 Book/Online Audio $12.99

BOOK 2

Book Two also includes: easy-to-follow tablature; fingerpicking; sixteenth notes; triplets; major scale; basic music theory; the minor pentatonic scale; add and sus chords; lead licks; Travis picking; 6/8 time; using a capo; and more! Also includes nearly 80 riffs and songs with online audio demos of every example.

00131207 Book/Online Audio $12.99

HAL LEONARD LEFT-HANDED BASS TAB METHOD BOOK 1

by Eric W. Wills

Now left-handed players can learn everything there is to know about beginning bass guitar with riffs like "Day Tripper," "Billie Jean," and "With or Without You." Book 1 includes: parts of the bass, easy-to-follow tablature, notes & riffs starting on the low E string, tempo & time signatures, understanding notes and rests, proper fingering and technique, slides and slurs, hammer-ons and pull-offs, many music styles, nearly 100 riffs and songs, audio CD with demos of every example, and more!

00151140 Book/Online Audio $12.99

HAL LEONARD BASS TAB METHOD

by Eric W. Wills

Learn everything there is to know about beginning bass guitar with riffs like "Day Tripper," "Billie Jean," and "With or Without You." Book 1 includes: parts of the bass, easy-to-follow tablature, notes & riffs starting on the low E string, tempo & time signatures, understanding notes and rests, proper fingering and technique, slides and slurs, hammer-ons and pull-offs, many music styles, nearly 100 riffs and songs, audio CD with demos of every example, and more!

00113068 Book/CD Pack $12.99

BOOK 2

This innovative method for electric bass guitar picks up where Book One leaves off. Learn notes up the fretboard with riffs like "Sunshine of Your Love" and "Sweet Emotion," scales with songs by Ozzy Osbourne and R.E.M., beginning slap technique with songs like "Panic Station" and "Higher Ground," and much more. The accompanying online audio features demos of all 69 riffs and songs in the book.

00124754 Book/Online Audio $12.99

SONGBOOK 1

Here are 10 hit songs tabbed for beginning guitarists to play while they are working through the Hal Leonard Bass Tab Method, or any other method. The songs are all on facing pages for no page turns, and the CD features both examples of how the guitar should sound, and full-band backing tracks so students can play the lead! The songs include: Beverly Hills • Born Under a Bad Sign • Brown Eyed Girl • Crazy Train • Hey Joe • I Won't Back Down • Smoke on the Water • Stir It Up • Use Somebody • You Are the Sunshine of My Life.

00120236 Book/CD Pack $12.99

7777 W. Bluemound Rd. P.O. Box 13819 Milwaukee, WI 53213
www.halleonard.com

Prices, contents, and availability subject to change without notice.

RECORDED VERSIONS®

The Best Note-For-Note Transcriptions Available

AUTHENTIC TRANSCRIPTIONS WITH NOTES AND TABLATURE

14037551 AC/DC – Backtracks $32.99
00690178 Alice in Chains – Acoustic $19.95
00694865 Alice in Chains – Dirt $19.95
00690958 Duane Allman Guitar Anthology $24.99
00694932 Allman Brothers Band – Volume 1 $24.95
00694933 Allman Brothers Band – Volume 2 $24.95
00694934 Allman Brothers Band – Volume 3 $24.95
00123558 Arctic Monkeys – AM $22.99
00690609 Audioslave $19.95
00690820 Avenged Sevenfold – City of Evil $24.95
00691065 Avenged Sevenfold – Waking the Fallen $22.99
00123140 The Avett Brothers Guitar Collection $22.99
00690503 Beach Boys – Very Best of $19.95
00690489 Beatles – 1 $24.99
00694832 Beatles – For Acoustic Guitar $22.99
00691014 Beatles Rock Band $34.99
00694914 Beatles – Rubber Soul $22.99
00694863 Beatles – Sgt. Pepper's Lonely Hearts Club Band $22.99
00110193 Beatles – Tomorrow Never Knows $22.99
00690110 Beatles – White Album (Book 1) $19.95
00691043 Jeff Beck – Wired $19.99
00692385 Chuck Berry $22.99
00690835 Billy Talent $19.95
00147787 Best of the Black Crowes $19.99
00690901 Best of Black Sabbath $19.95
14042759 Black Sabbath – 13 $19.99
00690831 blink-182 – Greatest Hits $19.95
00148544 Michael Bloomfield Guitar Anthology $24.99
00158600 Joe Bonamassa – Blues of Desperation $22.99
00690913 Boston $19.95
00690491 David Bowie – Best of $19.95
00690873 Breaking Benjamin – Phobia $19.95
00141446 Best of Lenny Breau $19.99
00690451 Jeff Buckley – Collection $24.95
00690957 Bullet for My Valentine – Scream Aim Fire $22.99
00691159 The Cars – Complete Greatest Hits $22.99
00691079 Best of Johnny Cash $22.99
00690590 Eric Clapton – Anthology $29.95
00690415 Clapton Chronicles – Best of Eric Clapton $18.95
00690936 Eric Clapton – Complete Clapton $29.99
00694869 Eric Clapton – Unplugged $22.95
00138731 Eric Clapton & Friends – The Breeze $22.99
00690162 The Clash – Best of $19.95
00101916 Eric Church – Chief $22.99
00690828 Coheed & Cambria – Good Apollo I'm Burning Star, IV, Vol. 1: From Fear Through the Eyes of Madness $19.95
00141704 Jesse Cook – Works Vol. 1 $19.99
00127184 Best of Robert Cray $19.99
00690819 Creedence Clearwater Revival – Best of $22.95
00690648 The Very Best of Jim Croce $19.95
00690613 Crosby, Stills & Nash – Best of $22.95
00691171 Cry of Love – Brother $22.99
00690967 Death Cab for Cutie – Narrow Stairs $22.99
00690289 Deep Purple – Best of $19.99
00690784 Def Leppard – Best of $22.99
00692240 Bo Diddley $19.99
00122443 Dream Theater $24.99
14041903 Bob Dylan for Guitar Tab $19.99
00139220 Tommy Emmanuel – Little by Little $24.99
00691186 Evanescence $22.99
00691181 Five Finger Death Punch – American Capitalist $22.99
00690664 Fleetwood Mac – Best of $19.95
00690870 Flyleaf $19.95
00690808 Foo Fighters – In Your Honor $19.95
00691115 Foo Fighters – Wasting Light $22.99
00690805 Robben Ford – Best of $22.99
00120220 Robben Ford – Guitar Anthology $24.99
00694920 Free – Best of $19.95
00690943 The Goo Goo Dolls – Greatest Hits Volume 1: The Singles $22.95
00691190 Best of Peter Green $19.99
00113073 Green Day – ¡Uno! $21.99
00116846 Green Day – ¡Dos! $21.99
00118259 Green Day – ¡Tré! $21.99
00694854 Buddy Guy – Damn Right, I've Got the Blues $19.95
00690840 Ben Harper – Both Sides of the Gun $19.95
00694798 George Harrison – Anthology $19.95
00690841 Scott Henderson – Blues Guitar Collection $19.95
00692930 Jimi Hendrix – Are You Experienced? $24.95
00692931 Jimi Hendrix – Axis: Bold As Love $22.95
00692932 Jimi Hendrix – Electric Ladyland $24.95
00690017 Jimi Hendrix – Live at Woodstock $24.95
00690602 Jimi Hendrix – Smash Hits $24.99
00119619 Jimi Hendrix – People, Hell and Angels $22.99
00691152 West Coast Seattle Boy: The Jimi Hendrix Anthology $29.99
00691332 Jimi Hendrix – Winterland (Highlights) $22.99
00690793 John Lee Hooker Anthology $24.99
00121961 Imagine Dragons – Night Visions $22.99
00690688 Incubus – A Crow Left of the Murder $19.95
00690790 Iron Maiden Anthology $24.99
00690684 Jethro Tull – Aqualung $19.95
00690814 John5 – Songs for Sanity $19.95
00690751 John5 – Vertigo $19.95
00122439 Jack Johnson – From Here to Now to You $22.99
00690271 Robert Johnson – New Transcriptions $24.95
00699131 Janis Joplin – Best of $19.95
00690427 Judas Priest – Best of $22.99
00120814 Killswitch Engage – Disarm the Descent $22.99
00124869 Albert King with Stevie Ray Vaughan – In Session $22.99
00694903 Kiss – Best of $24.95
00690355 Kiss – Destroyer $16.95
00690834 Lamb of God – Ashes of the Wake $19.95
00690875 Lamb of God – Sacrament $19.95
00114563 The Lumineers $22.99
00690955 Lynyrd Skynyrd – All-Time Greatest Hits $22.99
00694954 Lynyrd Skynyrd – New Best of $19.95
00690754 Marilyn Manson – Lest We Forget $19.95
00694956 Bob Marley– Legend $19.95
00694945 Bob Marley– Songs of Freedom $24.95
00139168 Pat Martino – Guitar Anthology $24.99
00129105 John McLaughlin Guitar Tab Anthology $24.99
00120080 Don McLean – Songbook $19.95
00694951 Megadeth – Rust in Peace $22.95
00691185 Megadeth – Th1rt3en $22.99
00690951 Megadeth – United Abominations $22.99
00690505 John Mellencamp – Guitar Collection $19.95
00690646 Pat Metheny – One Quiet Night $19.95
00690558 Pat Metheny – Trio: 99>00 $24.99
00118836 Pat Metheny – Unity Band $22.99
00690040 Steve Miller Band – Young Hearts $19.95
00119338 Ministry Guitar Tab Collection $24.99
00102591 Wes Montgomery Guitar Anthology $24.99
00691070 Mumford & Sons – Sigh No More $22.99
00151195 Muse – Drones $19.99
00694883 Nirvana – Nevermind $19.95
00690026 Nirvana – Unplugged in New York $19.95
00690807 The Offspring – Greatest Hits $19.95
00694847 Ozzy Osbourne – Best of $22.95
00690399 Ozzy Osbourne – Ozzman Cometh $22.99
00690933 Best of Brad Paisley $22.95
00690995 Brad Paisley – Play: The Guitar Album $24.99
00694855 Pearl Jam – Ten $22.99
00690439 A Perfect Circle – Mer De Noms $19.95
00690499 Tom Petty – Definitive Guitar Collection $19.95
00121933 Pink Floyd – Acoustic Guitar Collection $22.99
00690428 Pink Floyd – Dark Side of the Moon $19.95
00690789 Poison – Best of $19.95
00694975 Queen – Greatest Hits $24.95
00690670 Queensryche – Very Best of $19.95
00109303 Radiohead Guitar Anthology $24.99
00694910 Rage Against the Machine $19.95
00119834 Rage Against the Machine – Guitar Anthology $22.99
00690055 Red Hot Chili Peppers – Blood Sugar Sex Magik $19.95
00690584 Red Hot Chili Peppers – By the Way $19.95
00691166 Red Hot Chili Peppers – I'm with You $22.99
00690852 Red Hot Chili Peppers –Stadium Arcadium $24.95
00690511 Django Reinhardt – Definitive Collection $19.95
00690779 Relient K – MMHMM $19.95
14043417 Rodrigo y Gabriela – 9 Dead Alive $19.99
00690631 Rolling Stones – Guitar Anthology $27.95
00694976 Rolling Stones – Some Girls $22.95
00690264 The Rolling Stones – Tattoo You $19.95
00690685 David Lee Roth – Eat 'Em and Smile $19.95
00690942 David Lee Roth and the Songs of Van Halen $19.95
00151826 Royal Blood $22.99
00690031 Santana's Greatest Hits $19.95
00128870 Matt Schofield Guitar Tab Collection $22.99
00690566 Scorpions – Best of $22.95
00690604 Bob Seger – Guitar Collection $22.99
00138870 Ed Sheeran – X $19.99
00690803 Kenny Wayne Shepherd Band – Best of $19.95
00151178 Kenny Wayne Shepherd – Ledbetter Heights (20th Anniversary Edition) $19.99
00122218 Skillet – Rise $22.99
00691114 Slash – Guitar Anthology $24.99
00690813 Slayer – Guitar Collection $19.95
00120004 Steely Dan – Best of $24.95
00694921 Steppenwolf – Best of $22.95
00690655 Mike Stern – Best of $19.95
00690520 Styx Guitar Collection $19.95
00120081 Sublime $19.95
00120122 Sublime – 40oz. to Freedom $19.95
00690767 Switchfoot – The Beautiful Letdown $19.95
00690993 Taylor Swift – Fearless $22.99
00142151 Taylor Swift – 1989 $22.99
00115957 Taylor Swift – Red $21.99
00690531 System of a Down – Toxicity $19.95
00694824 James Taylor – Best of $17.99
00690871 Three Days Grace – One-X $19.95
00150209 Trans-Siberian Orchestra Guitar Anthology $19.99
00123862 Trivium – Vengeance Falls $22.99
00690683 Robin Trower – Bridge of Sighs $19.95
00660137 Steve Vai – Passion & Warfare $24.95
00110385 Steve Vai – The Story of Light $22.99
00690116 Stevie Ray Vaughan – Guitar Collection $24.95
00660058 Stevie Ray Vaughan – Lightnin' Blues 1983-1987 $24.95
00694835 Stevie Ray Vaughan – The Sky Is Crying $22.95
00690015 Stevie Ray Vaughan – Texas Flood $19.95
00152161 Doc Watson – Guitar Anthology $22.99
00690071 Weezer (The Blue Album) $19.95
00690966 Weezer – (Red Album) $19.99
00691941 The Who – Acoustic Guitar Collection $22.99
00690447 The Who – Best of $24.95
00122303 Yes Guitar Collection $22.99
00690916 The Best of Dwight Yoakam $19.95
00691020 Neil Young – After the Gold Rush $22.99
00691019 Neil Young – Everybody Knows This Is Nowhere $19.99
00691021 Neil Young – Harvest Moon $22.99
00690905 Neil Young – Rust Never Sleeps $19.99
00690623 Frank Zappa – Over-Nite Sensation $22.99
00121684 ZZ Top – Early Classics $24.99
00690589 ZZ Top Guitar Anthology $24.95

Prices and availability subject to change without notice.
Some products may not be available outside the U.S.A.

0516